HOW TO LOVE IN SANSKRIT

Praise for *How to Love in Sanskrit*

'Witty, surprising and joyous, this book banishes notions of solemnity and turgid scholarship that one might nurse about translations from the Sanskrit. Several translations here wear their learning lightly, as good poems must, reminding us that centuries are separated "by historians, not poets". A book to pick up, a book to gift.'

– Arundhathi Subramaniam

'This is a beautiful book, with wonderful contemporary translations of love poetry in Sanskrit (with some in Prakrit). The translations will charm and entice readers to read the originals. A difficult book to write, but since the two editors wear their scholarship lightly, they make it seem easy. A book that will delight the reader.'

– Bibek Debroy

HOW TO

Edited and Translated by

LOVE IN

Anusha Rao & Suhas Mahesh

SANSKRIT

Poems

HARPERPERENNIAL

An Imprint of HarperCollins *Publishers*

First published in English in India by Harper Perennial 2024
An imprint of HarperCollins *Publishers*
4th Floor, Tower A, Building No. 10, DLF Cyber City,
DLF Phase II, Gurugram, Haryana – 122002
www.harpercollins.co.in

2 4 6 8 10 9 7 5 3 1

P-ISBN: 978-93-5699-980-0
E-ISBN: 978-93-5699-808-7

Typeset in 11.5/16.2 Times New Roman at
Manipal Technologies Limited, Manipal

Printed and bound at
Thomson Press (India) Ltd

FSC
www.fsc.org
MIX
Paper from
responsible sources
FSC® C010615

This book is produced from independently certified FSC® paper
to ensure responsible forest management.

Contents

Introduction

You've probably done a little Sanskrit in school, learnt a few prayers at home, or at least heard them somewhere. What do you think of Sanskrit? The fusty-musty language of hymns, priests and godmen? Here's a surprise for you: love has been the overwhelming obsession of Sanskrit poets for over two thousand years. Fling a mean barb in a lover's quarrel? Brew a love potion? Turn someone crimson with a compliment? You're in luck. They've done all the hard work for you – grace, sophistication and wit included. We know of high Victorian romance with its strict etiquette, romantic letters and ballroom dances, brought to life in so many period dramas and novels. Love in Urdu with its intoxication, melancholy and madness is only too popular in the subcontinent. But what is it like to love in Sanskrit?

Love in Sanskrit is when you first laid eyes on him and it felt like an arrow struck you right in the heart. Had you lived till that moment? You weren't sure. Would you live again? You weren't sure. Your heart secretly bubbled and simmered on the inside, like a wet log on the hearth. A friend spilled the beans to him. You met by the lonely thickets on the riverbank. Sometimes you had entire conversations with your eyes because your parents were around. When he had to go away, the one little choked sob you gave while saying goodbye sliced right through his heart. You couldn't stop missing him. You wrote him a letter. The words weren't important; the smudge of the kohl that flowed with your tears spoke more eloquently. He was alone in his agony too. When the doe in the woods gave him a shy glance, he thought of your eyes. The rumble of the rain clouds felt like a weight in his chest. He thought it would drive him to insanity when the air turned dense with the fragrance of the ketaka blossoms, so dense that he could cup his palms and drink it in. You tossed and turned, praying for cursed sleep so you could at least dream of him in peace. When he finally returned, you kept it a secret so you could have him all to yourself for a day. Once you fought and resolutely refused to look at each other, but your eyes met, and you both burst into laughter. When you felt his goosebumps as you held his hand at your wedding. When he reached for your blouse and found it unhooked already as you pulled him close. When he woke up in the morning and saw your tousled hair and thought you looked even lovelier than the night before. And after a lifetime of sharing all joy and grief, when he died, you felt like he was saved, and you, in fact, were dead.

Like all great literature, Sanskrit tells us something about love by typifying its farthest possible extremes. It is about the cruel hand of fate. It is about ecstatic lovemaking. It is about clever flattery and quarrels of passion. But more than anything else, it is about yearning at its extreme. Mad yearning that strikes you like thunder, seizes you with frenzy, and drowns you in grief. We have an uneasy relationship with such grief today. It is to be medicated away, or kept muzzled except in solitude. In Sanskrit though, yearning is what nourishes love's plant and makes it burst into flower. Shared experiences of grief connect us, challenge us, and enrich us. As one poet asks: if you're not yearning, is it really love?

None have escaped heartbreak or grief, and you will discover that the old Indian heart is quite similar to Chinese, American or Indian hearts today. But the particular fashion in which romance plays out can be puzzling to the modern mind. To give you an extreme example, consider death. In Sanskrit, the death of your lover may not be a permanent tragedy, but a mere glitch in the timeline that will be corrected by reuniting in a future rebirth. The most acclaimed prose novel in Sanskrit, *Princess Kadambari,* kills off two main characters midway through the story, but brings them back in a different timeline for a happy ending.

We can also now tackle the question we're frequently asked: how do you say I love you in Sanskrit? The answer is simple. You don't say *I love you* in Sanskrit. It is simply not the way the Sanskritic mind does things. One way is to dispatch a close friend with a love letter containing a soppy poem you've written. This is what Shakuntala does in Kalidasa's *Recognition of Shakuntala:*

> I can't read your heart, cruel one.
> But as I long for you
> love sets every bit of me on fire
> day and night.

Or if you're absolutely sure they like you, you could offer them help with something, cheekily remarking that you're happy to put in 'every bodily effort'. Chandrapida does something like this in *Princess Kadambari*. In other words, Sanskrit resists linearity and matter-of-factness. Remember that this is a language in which you can open conversations with: *What letters are lucky enough to be a part of your name?* If you still insist on a literal translation, we prefer *tvayi sānurāgāsmi* (*tvayi sānurāgo 'smi* if you're a man).

This book is an invitation to Sanskrit love poetry in the way that an invitation to tea is an invitation to tea, biscuits and pakoras. Of the 200-odd entries in this book, around 150 are Sanskrit, around fifty are Maharashtri Prakrit, a couple in Apabhramsha, and one is Pali. All four are closely linked languages, and the first three are part of the same literary culture. This introduction is too short to elaborate further, but we will say this much: Maharashtri Prakrit and Apabhramsha were important classical languages of India, in use till the 1700s, but largely forgotten today. Maharashtri Prakrit's *Seven Hundred Gahas* (*Gāhāsattasaī*), which contains seven hundred vignettes on love, is one of the crowning glories of Indian literature. For nearly two thousand years, it was read all across India and held up as an exemplar of what poetry should aspire to be. The work's fame branded Maharashtri Prakrit as the ideal language for love – soft, tender and delicate – as opposed to abrasive Sanskrit which 'pops and crackles like a house of bamboo on fire'. Prakrit has not many takers today, but we maintain that it is worth learning Prakrit just to read *Seven Hundred Gahas*.

Some of the poems in this book come from the most celebrated writers of old India, such as Kalidasa and Banabhatta, whose works must have been feted with a procession on a royal elephant, as was custom. Many more are from lesser-known but very skilled writers such as Shivasvami, Sudhindra Tirtha and Uddyotana Suri. Some authors were card-carrying poets, some scholars, some emperors, some Buddhist, some Jain monks, some Hindu sanyasis, and many anonymous. We know of at least fifty women poets and two of them – Reva and Vidya – may be in this collection, though authorships are tricky to confirm.

These poems have been selected keeping the general reader in mind – no special knowledge or footnotes are needed to enjoy them. Nevertheless, even those who have spent a lifetime on Sanskrit will likely find things here that they have never seen before. A few verses also come from contemporary award-winners like Delhi University's Balram Shukla and Bengaluru's Shatavadhani Ganesh. Though numbers have declined, enthusiasm has not – Sanskrit love poetry continues to be written, and one of us even occasionally attends a poets' congress where participants spontaneously compose and recite verses, not unlike Bhoja's or Krishnadevaraya's court.

There is a well-established, traditional Sanskrit way of grouping verses together into chapters to form a collection. Some typical chapters might be 'Upset Lover', 'Youthful Charms', 'Lovemaking' and 'Moonrise'. Our chapter titles are more contemporary: 'How to Flirt', 'How to Quarrel', 'How to Let Go' and the like. The how-tos are not to be interpreted literally – very few of the verses offer explicit advice. The idea is to enjoy love depicted in its many hues, rather than through dry textbook instruction.

As modern readers, we may feel an impulse to project the concerns and fascinations of our world on to these old poems. We advise some caution in this regard. You may read a poem in which an innocent village girl pours out her feelings, but that doesn't mean an innocent village girl *actually* composed it. Anticlimactic, we know, but these are carefully calculated compositions by educated poets at royal courts and centres of learning. Similarly, consider poignant verses that are addressed to a lover. They were probably not addressed to any real person. The writing of Sanskrit poetry was rarely personal. These poems are technical masterpieces written to earn the appreciation and applause of audiences, and especially of competing poets.

Furthermore, Sanskrit poetry is like a magic mirror that continues to reflect practices that have long since vanished, and in some cases never existed in the first place. Writers regularly take inspiration from writers that came hundreds of years before them. A poet in Kashmir may write about lovers on the banks of the Godavari, having seen neither the Godavari nor such lovers but being inspired by the *Seven Hundred Gahas*. Was India some kind of hippie wonderland? Did women have as much agency as we see in these poems? How did gender dynamics work? These poems cannot answer such questions of history for us. And why should they have to?

What can the reader get out of this book then? The Sanskrit tradition obliges us to declare this up front. Enjoyment, of course. There are lessons here, too, though only few are explicitly stated. Tradition tells us that poetry teaches like a lover, subtle and undemanding, but gently persuasive. As a couple who spends a lot of time reading old literature, its impact on us has been total and irrevocable. Once Anusha, without explanation, shipped a pair of kohl-stained earrings across the Atlantic (see verse 104) to Suhas and received a blank sheet of paper (see below) in response from him. No words were exchanged, but the message was clear.

biraha bikala binu hī likhī pātī daī paṭhāi
āṃka bihūnīyau sucita sūnai bāṃcatu jāi

She was in such a daze
she sent him a wordless letter.
He was in such a daze
he read it with rapt attention.

– *Bihari's Seven Hundred 314* (Brajbhasha),
Bihari Lal, 1600 CE

At home, we speak a melange of Kannada, English, Sanskrit and Prakrit, and frequently quote and adapt lines from our favourite verses in everyday conversation. We write each other verses of appreciation, argument and apology in the classical style. We do a great deal more. These poems reveal to us a different world where we can be creative, candid, and willing to feel. A world where love creates art and literature, not customized trinkets. A world that wants to give and receive love, not just branded markers of love. Such is the world these poems inhabit, and you too can be a part of that world.

A Tour of the Translators' Workshop

A Sanskrit poem is like an Indian wedding – people flit about in glitzy clothing, raucous children mill all around, horses neigh, bells tintinnabulate, priests chant and food beckons. It may not even be clear who the bride and groom are, unless you know where to look. Every now and then, some long-forgotten word or expression pops up, like some ancient elder, and you shake their gnarly hands and try your best to hold a conversation.

The Sanskrit translator's job is to take it and replan it as a solemn church wedding in England. You could probably serve samosas without a kerfuffle, but you will be thought mad if you trot down the aisle on a horse. In short, translation is largely a game of compromise. Luckily, translators of exotic languages, especially poetry, have a secret advantage.

Most readers cannot stand to look ignorant and will only nod sagely at the exotic book they just purchased. Surely it must mean something profound, even if it makes no sense to them. Even better, it must mean something profound *because* it makes no sense to them. We do not wish for us to be that translator, or for you to be that reader. There are a few reasons why a translation may make little sense to the general reader. Here is Exhibit A, an unfortunate translation of *Seven Hundred Gahas 48* by a well-regarded Indian scholar of the previous century:

> *O deity! be pleased to ordain for our beloved (one) an addiction to other women, for, male persons, who enjoy the love of one (female) person, cannot discriminate between merits and demerits (of women).*

This idea can carry well into English, and the translator clearly understood it, but preferred to communicate in hieroglyphs. We diagnose this as a case of excessive attention to irrelevant detail. A photographer should know that the shehnai and fireworks are not as important as the bride and groom. Alternatively, translating Sanskrit into English for the general reader can be thought of as an exercise in minimalism: how do you ignore all the flourishes and filigrees, while essentially painting the same picture? Here is our translation (v. 111):

Dear God,
make him hang out
with other women more.
He does not seem to realize
what a catch I am.

Our Exhibit B is a verse from the Ramayana, jointly translated by two Americans – one scholar and one poet – in a collection of poems that enjoyed wide circulation:

cañcac-candra-kara-sparśa-harṣonmīlita-tārakā
aho! rāgavatī sandhyā jahāti svayam ambaram

Red also in love twilight
at the hands of moon
her lover

stars her eyes wide at his touch

oh

happily she abandons
dress and sky.

This complex verse has not one, but four plays on words that all fit together like a picture puzzle. Here, *kara* is ray/

hand, *tārakā* is star/pupil, *rāga* is redness/love, and *ambara* is sky/dress. The translation fails to convey any real idea, but sounds vaguely lyrical, like the output of some poetry-writing AI program. We diagnose this as a case of bad curation. Indeed, it is impossible to translate such poetry for general audiences; the magic dissipates in the process.

Wordplay aside, there is a still more serious problem: the great cultural distance. Just as the average Englishman today lacks the background to appreciate Shakespeare's references to Greek mythology, the average Indian does not grasp the conceptual universe that India inhabited before colonization. How can we window-gazers know that young mango leaves glow a delicate red before they mature into green? Or that moonlit nights, usually cool as a balm, can feel like a firebrand if you're missing him? We all know the Bollywood trope of romance in the rain, but do we know that the rumblings of the interminable Indian monsoon sound like death's drum when your lover is away? Sometimes imagery is deeply problematic or decidedly unromantic to the modern reader. Would your girlfriend be flattered if you compared her thighs to the trunk of an elephant? These things were once perfectly intuitive but are impossible to understand today without reams of footnotes. They are often the raw material from which more complex poetry is built.

Thus, though a ship's worth of Sanskrit poetry has survived, only a bucket's worth has potential in English. The success of a book of translations hinges less on the translator's skill and more on curatorship. The translator has to be willing (and equipped) to read through thousands of poems to find the few hundred champions, much like a pharma company tests thousands of compounds to find that one winning drug. Here, existing books disappoint. They consult the same half-a-dozen sources, filter insufficiently, and often produce baffling translations that cannot be enjoyed but only gawked at like exotic animals in a zoo. The 200 or so verses in this book were selected after examining over 10,000 verses from over 150 Sanskrit and Prakrit works (see appendix for a list), many nearly forgotten.

Our final exhibit is *Seven Hundred Gahas 617,* taken from a recent translation by two able European scholars:

> I will do my best to avoid
> Doing the things you don't like,
> But, my dear,
> What can I do about the things
> I don't like?

While their language is very readable, we think the translators have missed the point. We diagnose this as a case of 'even Homer nods'. Here is our translation (v. 191):

> Anything that
> isn't to your liking,
> I won't do.

But tell me, darling,
what can I do
when the thing
that isn't to your liking
is me?

Sanskrit poetry is subtle, clever, even sneaky, and can present slippery ground for even those who spend a lifetime wrangling with it. As is apologetically said at the end of some manuscripts: even Bhima loses some fights; even sages sometimes get into a muddle. It is a statistical guarantee that any large translation project will objectively have a few errors. We do our best to avoid this by consulting old commentaries and modern scholarship, talking to experts, and being dissatisfied till we have *really* understood it. Given the antiquity of some of these poems though, some things are irretrievably lost. What *exactly* does *palala-guḍa-bāhya-vyatikaraiḥ* (v. 182) mean? Who knows? Write to us if you do. Fortunately, the number of such translators' allergens is rather small, perhaps only half a dozen in this book.

We shall now give you a demonstration of how we refit Sanskrit verses for modern English. Let us use *Treasury of Verse-Jewels 784* as a case study:

*netrendīvari**ṇī** mukhāmburuhi**ṇī** bhrū-valli-kallolin**ī***
*bāhu-dvandva-mṛṇālin**ī** yadi **vadhū**r vāpī punaḥ sā bhavet*
*tal-**lā**vaṇya-jal**ā**vagāhana-jaḍair **aṅgair** anaṅgānala-*
*jvālā-jāla-mucas tyajeyam asam**āḥ** prāṇa-cchido ve**danāḥ***

If she were but a pond
her eyes two lilies
her face a lotus
her slender arms lotus stalks
her dancing eyebrows ripples
I would plunge at once
into the cool waters of her loveliness
and be rid of this searing pain
that threatens to rip life from limb.

What do we do with the poetic metre? This is the first big question. Here, the metre is the majestic Tiger's Play (*śārdūlavikrīḍita*) and its complex texture has no English equivalent. In fact, metre itself has largely been abandoned in English. Of the many effects the rhythm of the Tiger's Play generates, our favourite is the sharp intake of breath it forces close to the end of the final line, mirroring the searing pain being spoken of. The harsh *cch* in *prāṇa-cchido* seems to summon the agony of having life ripped apart. Also note the many alliterations and internal rhymes marked in bold. The honest translator simply accepts that these effects do not translate into readable English. Even if they could be translated, would speakers of English perceive them at all, these melodies and rhythms from an alien tradition? Thus, we choose to focus on meaning, and say goodbye to metre and sound. Here is an English rendering that shows you how the Sanskrit actually works:

If the girl were a reservoir with
eyes-blue-lotuses
face-lotus
eyebrow-vine-waves
arm-lotus-stalks
I would give up these
bodiless-fire-flame-multitude-spewing
life-breath-cutting incomparable agonies
with my limbs
that are her-loveliness-water-immersion-cooled

This bewildering piece of text points us towards the second big problem: compound words, great processions of letters that march forth like armies, sometimes invading two lines at once. Long, sticky compound words like *tallāvaṇyajalāvagāhanajaḍair* (her-loveliness-water-submersion-cool) have to be remade into the powdery language that is English. There is yet another serious problem: metaphors. How can eyebrows be like vines? The same way hearts can be of gold. Metaphors are not plug-and-play across languages. Therefore, we ignore the vines and translate the wave with an equivalent for the image: *her dancing eyebrows ripples*. Reservoir sounds more like civil engineering than poetry, so we call it a pond. Who ever speaks of blue lotuses in English? We use the word lily instead. The word *asamāḥ* (incomparable) does not add much to the verse, so we leave it out.

After a few rounds of such polish, we may have arrived at something that faithfully translates the lovely *idea* behind the verse: seeing your lover reflected in nature, the intolerable pain of being apart, the idle fantasies of being together, and the visceral relief of cool water on a burn. These are the things the Sanskrit makes us feel, and these are the things we hope the translation will make you feel too.

Acknowledgements

Our first gratitude is to the authors of these and other wonderful verses, and centuries of hawk-eyed commentators, editors and scribes who kept them alive and gifted them to us. Many thanks to our incredible editor Rahul Soni, for seeing the promise in the book, as well as for his ideas, advice and edits. We have been lucky to have readers whom we hold in high esteem. Our gratitude to all our initial readers for their scholarly rigour, astute comments, and endless encouragement: Gratius Avitus, Shashi Kiran B.N., Raj Balkaran, Janani Comar, Bibek Debroy, Elisa Freschi, Anupama Kuttikat, Suma Nagaraj, Srilata Raman, Sandhya Ranganathan, Ajay Rao, Arundhathi Subramaniam, and René Verma. Our special thanks to Naresh Keerthi, Andrew Ollett, Shreevatsa R., and Nidhi Surendranath for their careful comments on every line of the translation – the book is all the richer with your help. We thank Mihir Arjunwadkar (son of Krishna S. Arjunawadkar), Shatavadhani Ganesh, G.S.S. Murthy and Balram Shukla for graciously allowing us to use their verses. Thanks also to Harunaga Isaacson for kindly sending over a copy of *Rasikajivana*.

We are grateful to Vanamala Viswanatha, who not only helped us find a home for this book at HarperCollins India, but also suggested some very pertinent edits. We thank our families for their love and support, and kindly request them to skip chapter VI.

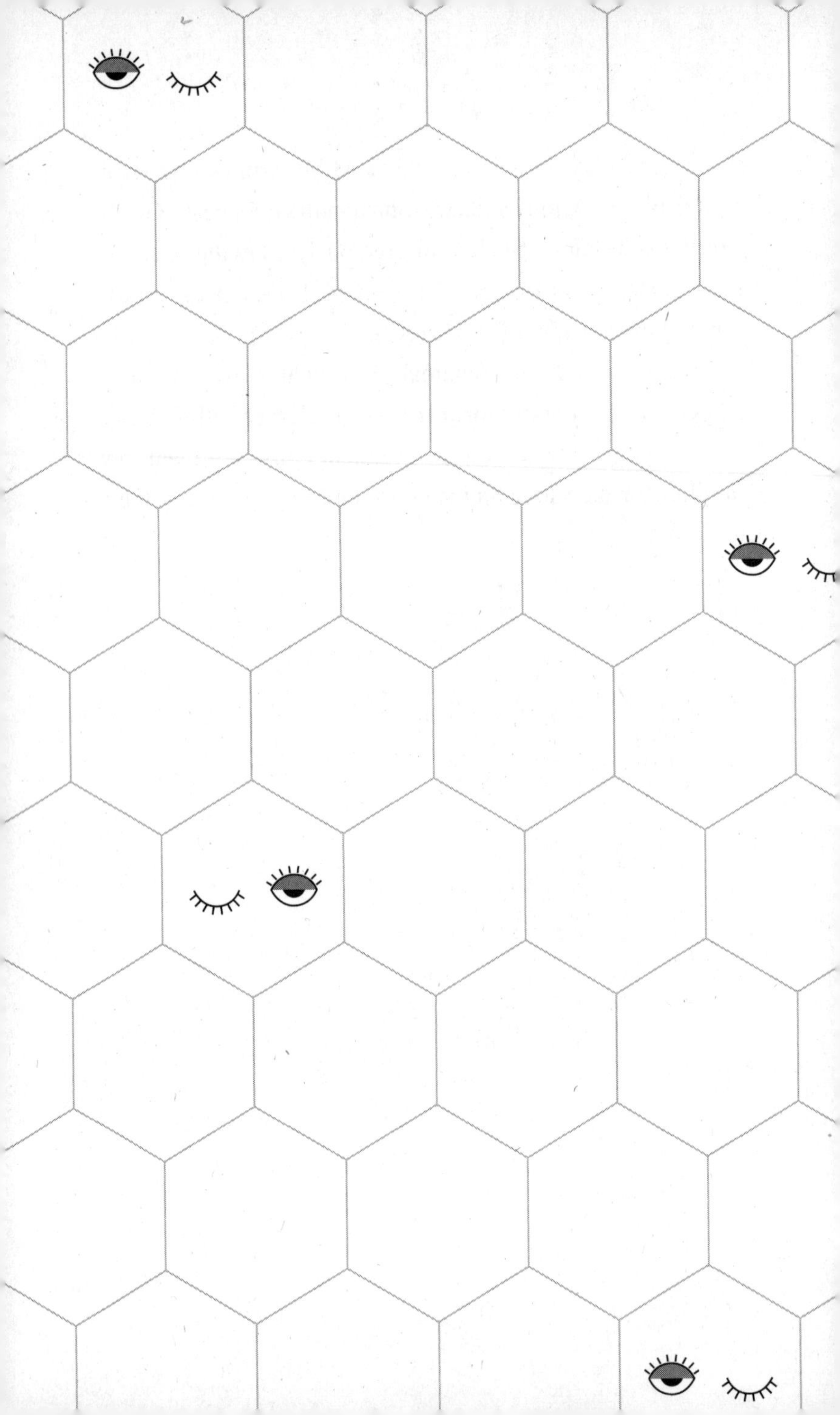

HOW TO FLIRT

1. Inferiority complex

Seeing the lovely red
of your lips, darling
the cherries hang themselves
from a tree in despair.

Kumarapala's Awakening, Somaprabha Suri, 1200 CE, Gurjara

Who do you think wrote this gem of a verse? A young romantic? It was actually the Jain monk Somaprabha Suri.

2. Prolonging the moment

As the girl at the well
pours out water
making it trickle thin
and thinner still,
the traveller bends,
eyes upwards
sipping the water
through cupped hands
spreading his fingers wide
and wider still.

Seven Hundred Gahas, 100 CE?, Deccan

This verse went viral in old India. Umpteen other works across languages quote it and imitate it.

3. Why I am an atheist

When the creator made her

if he had his eyes open
would he have let her leave heaven?
Surely not.

If he had his eyes shut
could he have achieved such perfection?
No chance.

Therefore it is proved
that the Buddha was right:
There is no creator.

Treasury of Verse-Jewels, 1000 CE, Bengal

This verse is attributed to Dharmakirti, a heavyweight of Buddhist philosophy. By some accounts, he was based at the great monastic university of Nalanda (now in Bihar).

4. Logician's quandary

Clearly it's impossible that
the same undiscerning god
who made all manner of things –
good, bad, and ugly
could have created you.

Shall we hypothesize a new god then?
But how would someone so inexperienced
handle such a task?

Was it a happy accident,
like worms tracing letters
as they nibble through leaves?
No way.

And so
all the logicians
find themselves in a muddle
about how you came to be.

Bhartrisarasvata's Anthology, Bhartrisarasvata, 1000 CE, Kashmir

5. Dimples

After creating her
God must have
gazed at his work admiringly
holding her face in his hands
thumb on each cheek.

That's how she got
her two perfect dimples.

Deeds of the Nishadha King, Shriharsha, 1100 CE, Kanyakubja?

Some say that *Deeds of the Nishadha King* is the most challenging poem in Sanskrit.

6. Dangerous driving

First her high breasts
then the deep valley
of her waist
then the steep incline
of her hips –

with all these
curves and bends
is it a surprise
that every onlooker
goes off track?

Sharngadhara's Anthology, 1300 CE, Ranthambore

7. Can't take my eyes off you

On whatever bit of her
the gaze first lands,
there it stays pinned.

No one knows her
in all her loveliness.

Seven Hundred Gahas, 100 CE?, Deccan

Seven Hundred Gahas is the most celebrated Prakrit work, written in a metrical form called the gaha. Many other well-known works are its imitations, such as Govardhana's *Arya Saptashati* (Sanskrit) and Bihari's *Satsai* (Brajbhasha).

8. When looks kill

The doctors say that only poison
can counteract poison.
Save my life –
look into my eyes again.

Ornament to Love

The cause of an illness was sometimes believed to also be its cure, just as it takes a thorn to remove a thorn.

9. Why deer live in the forest

Hoping for a boon
of eyes as lovely as yours
the deer have taken
to an ascetic life in the forest.

Kumarapala's Awakening, Somaprabha Suri, 1200 CE, Gurjara

10. Don't rub it in

Beautiful,
let your doe-eyes be.
No kohl, please.

When the arrow can kill by itself
why rub poison on the tip?

Enlivener of Connoisseurs, 1600 CE, Mithila

11. Miss Universe

The long bindi
painted on her forehead
pointing straight up to heaven

is the Love God's arrow
that he mounts
on the arched bow of her brows.

Earth has been won already.
Heaven must be next.

What Navasahasanka Did, Padmagupta, 1000 CE, Malwa

What Navasahasanka Did reimagines the author's patron as a hero who goes on fantastic adventures in many worlds.

12. Natural beauty

The arch of your brow
is a graceful vine.
Your rosy lips
newly blossoming buds.

Your face is a gorgeous garden.
Any other is just wilderness.

Joy of the Serpents, Harshavardhana, 600 CE, Kanyakubja

The poet is King Harshavardhana of Kannauj, who not only ruled most of northern India, but also wrote three plays that are now classics: *Ratnavali*, *Priyadarshika* and *Nagananda*.

13. Desperate measures

Sweetheart,
the moon has taken to penance.

He wastes away by the Ganga
in the thicket of Shiva's locks
desperate to be lovelier
than your lovely face.

Treasury of Verse-Jewels, 1000 CE, Bengal

Treasury of Verse-Jewels was compiled by a Buddhist monk, Vidyakara, who seems to have enjoyed collecting love verses rather more than religious ones.

14. Subtle compliments

Busy in the kitchen,
she brushed a sooty hand
across her face
and her husband grinned:
'Now your face looks like the moon!'

Seven Hundred Gahas, 100 CE?, Deccan

The moon is popularly understood to have a smudge on it – its dark spot, variously imagined to be a rabbit, a deer, and more recently as black money stashed by dead politicians gone to heaven. The subtext is that her face is usually even prettier than the moon.

15. No other like you

Time after time
hoping to match
the loveliness of your face
the creator builds the full moon
piece by piece.

And time after time
frustrated, wipes it off –
only to try again.

Seven Hundred Gahas, 100 CE?, Deccan

16. Don't be a nerd

All your pious reading
has ruined you.

Like the worm that
feasts on bitter neem leaves
you don't know
what's good for you.

We'll go to hell?
At least it'll be together.
Let's go for it.

Seven Hundred Gahas, 100 CE?, Deccan

17. Why won't you like me back?

How skilfully
the Love God launches his arrows!

He strikes me
squarely in the chest
but doesn't
so much as touch you
though you're right there
in my heart.

Ambrosial Ocean of Verse, 1300 CE, Karnata

Ambrosial Ocean of Verse was compiled by Sayana, brother of the highly revered Vidyaranya, who helped found the Vijayanagara Empire.

18. She knows best

She calls me hard-hearted. She should know. The moment I set eyes on her, she stole my heart and took it home with her.

Tales of Ten Young Men, Dandi, 700 CE?, Dravida

19. Tricks of the trade

'Look, darling
there's the thorn
clear as day.
Now draw it out
with your nails
but be gentle.'

She placed her foot
on his lap.

There was no thorn.

Sharngadhara's Anthology, 1300 CE, Ranthambore

Besides poetry, *Sharngadhara's Anthology* also contains much practical advice about such topics as archery, veterinary science, digging wells and medicine. If you've been poisoned, grind together pepper, salt, ghee, honey and neem fruits and eat the paste, he says, for it will purge you of the poison – from both ends.

20. Game theory

Desire works
in a backwards fashion:
If they're disinclined
you desire them more.
If they dance to your tunes
your desire slackens.

Therefore, if you want
the greatest pleasure
practise playing hard to get.

Heart's Delight, Someshvara, 1100 CE, Karnata

Heart's Delight is a thick encyclopaedia by King Someshvara III that includes (amongst other things), old recipes for idlis (idarika), vadas (vataka), dosas (dhosaka) and a variety of wines.

21. I won't be missing you, I'm afraid

My love, remember me.
Alas, I cannot do the same.
We remember with our hearts
and you have stolen mine.

Line-up of Good Verse, 1400 CE, Kashmir

Many sensitive readers of old made collections of their favourite verses, and some of these anthologies have come down to us. Of these, the Kashmiri *Line-up of Good Verse* is one of the largest, with 3,500 verses.

22. Tell me the secret

Pretty girl,
on which mountain
and with what technique
did your little parrot do his penance
that he now gets to
bite into this cherry
red as your lip?

Light on Suggestion, 800 CE, Kashmir

Light on Suggestion champions the idea that great poetry evokes moods through what its words suggest, rather than through their literal meaning.

23. Sophistication

‘I love you.
Why don’t you love me back?’
Such coarseness
will only worsen your case.

‘The Love God’s dratted arrows
have wounded me quite fatally.
I’m just thankful that
he leaves you in peace.’

Now that might get you somewhere.

Mirror of Poetry, Dandi, 700 CE?, Dravida

Mirror of Poetry was an old international bestseller, having been translated into a variety of languages including Tibetan and Mongolian.

24. Coming together

I am he, you are she.
You are verse, I am song.
I am heaven, you are earth.
Let us live as one
and bring children into this world.

Atharva Veda

This is a wedding hymn in the Atharva Veda.

25. I wasn't born yesterday

My child,
to whom are you
folding your hands in namaste?

Prayers to the gods
don't involve all these
smiles and stolen glances.

Seven Hundred Gahas, 100 CE?, Deccan

26. When lovers gamble

They played a game of dice.
A kiss was the stake.
Who won? Who lost?
How do we decide?
Could the Love God tell us?

I doubt even he knows.

Line-up of Good Verse, 1400 CE, Kashmir

27. Going all in

First
a hug was wagered
and won.
They played some more.
Lips were staked
and kisses won.

Then he asked her:
'What are you betting next?'

Cheeks thrilling
from hiding
her rising excitement
beads of sweat coating her hand
she moved her pawn
across the board
without a single word.

Treasury of Verse-Jewels, 1000 CE, Bengal

28. Playing to lose

'Yes, I staked my lips
and you won the round.
But that only means
you can have my lips.

Who are you
to break the rules
and take it a step further?'

With eyebrows raised
in playful anger
she held my face
and had her revenge
by doing something
far more precious
than anything I'd won.

Pearl Necklace of Verses, 1200 CE, Deccan

29. Boys' poker night

At their house
his friends have gathered,
and the boys' night is just
getting started.
She quietly walks
to the bedroom
letting her anklets tinkle
(just as her clever friends suggested).

To him it sounds like
the twang
of the Love God's bow.
All too eager
he feigns a yawn
and looks up at the boys:
'Shall we call it a night, then?'

The clock hasn't even struck nine.

Ambrosia for the Ears, 1200 CE, Bengal

30. Wise counsel

Gaze at him to your heart's content.
It's better than stealing glances.
That way, you'll get a good look
and onlookers will be sympathetic –
'The poor girl has no wiles.'

Seven Hundred Gahas, 100 CE?, Deccan

31. Marksmanship

She raises her left arm
and reaches back
to undo her brassiere.

It's like
she's reaching back
into a quiver
to draw an arrow
and shoot straight at his heart.

Enlivener of Connoisseurs, 1600 CE, Mithila

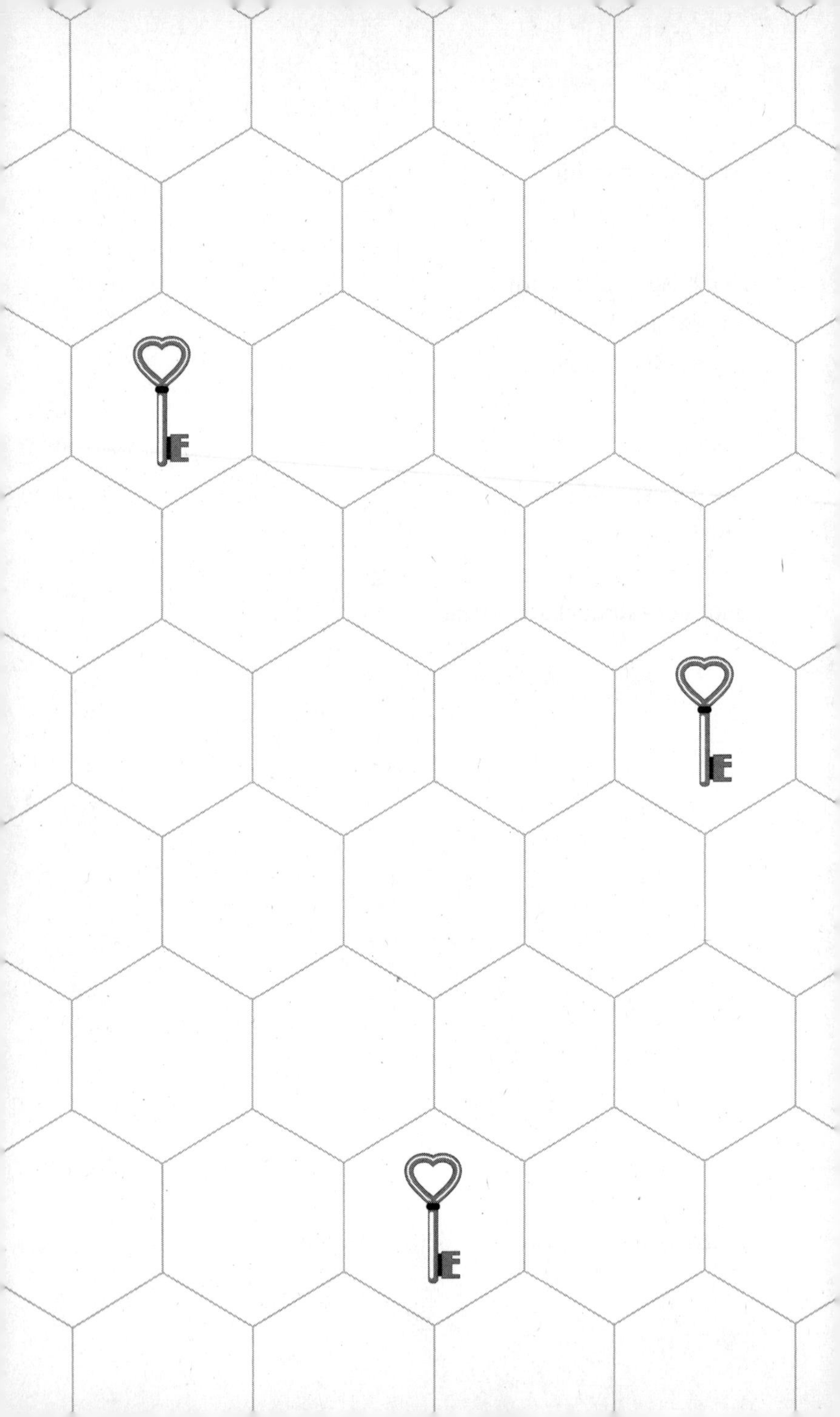

HOW TO KEEP IT A SECRET

32. Open secret

You can conceal many things.
Love, however, is different.
The harder you try to hush it up
the more painfully obvious it becomes.

Princess Lilavai, Kouhala, 800 CE

Princess Lilavai is a Prakrit romance centred around the Satavahana King Hala and Princess Lilavai of Simhala.

33. What gave it away?

When he came home
I didn't look at him
I didn't speak to him
I didn't offer him anything.

That's how they guessed.

Treasury of Gahas, 1000 CE

34. Air of mystery

Silly girl,
don’t reveal all in love.
Some things are shared
and some should stay mysteries.

Even Parvati
who shares half of herself
with her husband

only shares the half.

Suhas Mahesh, Contemporary, Bengaluru

35. Religious experience

When my next-door neighbour –
a fine lady, married, brazen,
worldly-wise, fun –
comes on to me
even the joy of moksha
feels as worthless
as blades of grass.

Seven Hundred Aryas, Govardhana, 1100 CE, Bengal

36. Well-kept secrets

I’m quite sure
that the thick reeds
by the river chuckled
with my ex-boyfriends
on my wedding day

listening to the
solemn recitation of hymns
blessing the virgin bride.

Seven Hundred Gahas, 100 CE?, Deccan

Secret affairs were often conducted by the riverbank, with reeds tall enough to guarantee the couple some privacy.

37. Kuch to log kahenge

Darling,
people like to talk.
But you can't give up love.

We worry about lice
but who stops wearing clothes?

Vidyakara Mishra's Thousand, 1800 CE

38. Stolen love

Lamps snuffed out.
Hushed breathing.
Shushed exchanges.
A hundred promises
to keep it secret.

Ah, the pleasures
of stolen lovemaking!

Seven Hundred Gahas, 100 CE?, Deccan

39. Parental controls

Riding the waves of new love
but held back by the embankment
of elders at home
they stand close
with unfulfilled longing
drinking
and drinking
each other in
with their eyes.

Amaru's Hundred, 600 CE?

A certain commentary 'demonstrates' how love poems from *Amaru's Hundred* can also be read as spiritual metaphors. This is done using grammatical tricks and clever redivisions of words. For instance, it may explain that 'I love you' is really 'Oh I! Love you(rself)' – a call to love the supreme spirit within yourself.

40. A day for rainbows

You remember that day
don't you, darling?
When you were leaving
to study in the big city
and we met under the banyan tree,
nervous about my dad.
Like a confused day
with sun and rain
I was all smiles and tears –
at once.

Husband and Wife Talk, G.S. Srinivasa Murthy, Contemporary, Bengaluru

Husband and Wife Talk traces the evolution of a couple's relationship all the way from high school to grandparenthood.

41. Second date

'When will we meet again, my dear?'

'If the holy books are right
I'm sure we'll run into each other
in hell.'

Heard Through the Oral Tradition

There are several hells, each specializing in a kind of sin. The specific hell referred to in this verse is the Deep Frier (Kumbhipaka), where sinners are cooked in vats of oil.

42. The trouble with being shy

Friends?
I can't trust them
to not blab.

The man I love?
I'm sure it's painfully obvious
to him
but I can't even look him
in the eye.

Townsfolk?
They're talented
at reading into every gesture
from a mile away
and making cruel jokes.

Whom can I turn to?

The fire of my love
was born in this heart
only to die there.

Amaru's Hundred, 600 CE?

There is a saying that Amaru packs into one verse what others express in entire books.

43. Polly wants a cracker

The pet parrot
begins to loudly squawk
before the elders of the house
repeating all it had heard
the night before.

The mortified girl
hastens to take off her ruby earring
and dangles it before the parrot
like it were a pomegranate seed,
bribing it into silence.

Amaru's Hundred, 600 CE?

This motif of a tattletale parrot repeating embarrassing conversations is a favourite of poets. A fine ivory carving of this scene can be seen in the Guimet Museum in Paris.

44. No chaperones, please

'Where do you tiptoe to
in this blinding darkness?'

'To meet my lover
dearer to me than life.'

'You're all alone.
Have you no fear?'

'I have the Love God
armed with his arrows
to escort me.'

Amaru's Hundred, 600 CE?

45. Window to the soul

Eyes turning slowly,
tender with love,
looking there one moment,
embarrassed, wavering,
back here the next.

Who is this lucky man
to whom your eyes
pour out the secrets
of your heart?

Amaru's Hundred, 600 CE?

46. Rumour mills

Forget chatting him up
or slipping him my number,
the rumour mills
churn in this little village
if I so much as sigh.

Treasury of Gahas, 1000 CE

The setting is some little village in what is Maharashtra today, somewhere on the banks of the Narmada or the Godavari.

47. Small-town troubles

The people in this gossipy little village
could fit an entire pestle
into a pinprick
with their tall tales.

We both live here
but I haven't dared
to even look him in the eye.

Seven Hundred Gahas, 100 CE?, Deccan

48. Eloquent silence

With people swirling all around
he could only speak to her
through eyes
that shone with delight.

She too replied
through limbs
that broke out in a sweat.

Seven Hundred Gahas, 100 CE?, Deccan

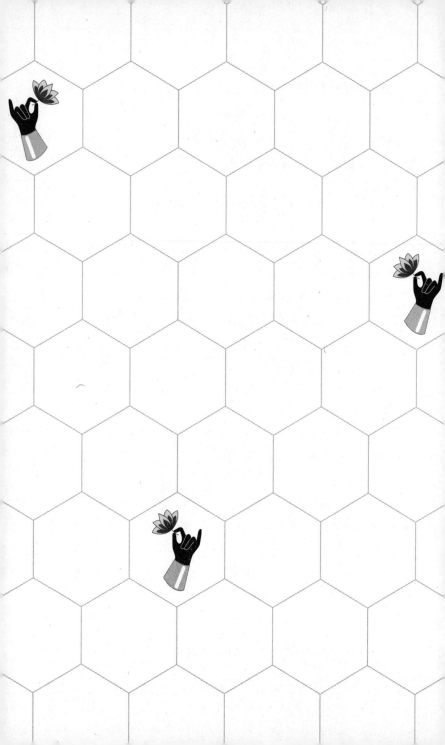

HOW TO DAYDREAM

49. Pearls and corals

A white blossom enfolded
in the blush of fresh shoots –

A pearl set
in flaming coral –

Only they might hint at the perfection
of her dazzling smile
and red lips.

Birth of Kumara, Kalidasa, 400 CE?

Through the story of how Shiva and Parvati came to be together, *Birth of Kumara* weaves together a series of meditations on the pursuit of love, inevitability, supreme divinity and the power of penance. Parvati stands out as an unusually strong lead.

50. Extrasensory perception

‘She does every little thing I like,’ he gushes.
Little does he know
he likes every little thing she does.

Light on Love, 1000 CE, Malwa

Light on Love goes so far as to argue that love is the *only* rasa or aesthetic sentiment.

51. Sui generis

In all the world
filled as it is with lovely women
this much may be said of her:
only her right half
is a match for her left.

Seven Hundred Gahas, 100 CE?, Deccan

52. Class topper

Vatsyayana (of *Kamasutra* fame),
Madanodaya, Dattaka,
Vitavritta, Rajaputra,
and all the other sexperts of yore –
forget what they wrote.

What they so much as breathed –
her heart knows it already.

Bawd's Counsel, Damodaragupta, 800 CE, Kashmir

The *Kamasutra* opens with a long listing of the erotic texts that came before it. It is said that the original *Kamasutra* (with a thousand chapters!) was written by Nandi. This material was reused by many authors to produce many derivative works. Finally, Vatsyayana wrote the small but comprehensive summary that we know as the *Kamasutra*.

53. In my heart

Has she melted into my heart?
Or is she reflected there?
Perhaps she's been painted?
Or engraved?
Or studded
like some precious gem?
Or consecrated
like a goddess on her plinth?
Or buried
like some invaluable treasure?
Or pinned
by the Love God's five arrows?
Or sewn tight
into the fabric of my heart
by the threads of my thoughts?

Malati and Madhava, Bhavabhuti, 700 CE, Kanyakubja

Bhavabhuti stands out among Sanskrit poets for his interest in depicting the stirrings of the mind.

54. Every time you touch me

It teeters on that edge
between pleasure and pain.
Is it a daze? A dream?
Poison swirling in my veins?
Or is it madness?

Your every touch
blurs my senses
with a numbing cold
and a searing heat
all at once.

What Rama Did Next, Bhavabhuti, 700 CE, Kanyakubja

What Rama Did Next is a brilliant exploration of morality, obligation and conscience through the episode of Rama's abandonment of Sita. It is one of the highest achievements of Sanskrit theatre.

55. Seal of approval

Her cherry lips look
like God's official seal
certifying her
as a treasury
of perfect loveliness.

Treasury of Gahas, 1000 CE

The king's seal used to be stamped in sindoor (vermilion), validating such matters as the payment of tax. We have slightly adapted the idea in translation.

56. I rest my case

The pearl necklace
bobs to the rhythm
of the girl's breasts.
If such is the fate of the cultured
what hope have the rest of us?

Treasury of Verse-Jewels, 1000 CE, Bengal

We have adapted the pun to make it work in English. Real pearls grown through human intervention are called cultured pearls.

57. Fiery passion

It is as if
the fire of passion
moves across
her body
apportioning itself:

As burning red
in her lips

As comforting warmth
in her breasts

As smoky darkness
in her lush hair

As fiery pride
in her heart

As sooty blackness
in her kohl

Ascent of King Kapphina, Shivasvami, 800 CE, Kashmir

As an aside, *Ascent of King Kapphina* performs an incredible feat of language: it has a chapter that can be simultaneously read in Sanskrit and Prakrit.

58. I carry your heart

Go
as far as you like
but my heart
will never let go of you.

Like at sunset
a tree's shadow
may grow apart
but does the root let go?

Wishing Tree of Rasa, 1700 CE, Bengal

Chaturbhuja Mishra compiled the *Wishing Tree of Rasa* under the patronage of Shaista Khan, the subedar of Mughal Bengal.

59. The things we do for love

She would startle
at the very mention of a snake.
Now the same Parvati
pats the snake on Shiva's arm
into her cushion as she sleeps.

What will we not do for love?

Seven Hundred Aryas, Govardhana, 1100 CE, Bengal

Govardhana was a friend of his more famous contemporary Jayadeva, author of the *Gita Govinda*. Jayadeva gives him high praise for having 'no equal when it comes to love poetry'.

60. Body art

Yes, my dear
we get it.
Your husband did
all that wonderful body art
on your breasts.

Mine would too

if only he could
hold his hands steady
when he's anywhere near me.

Seven Hundred Gahas, 100 CE?, Deccan

It was the fashion of the day to paint ornamental designs (patralekha) on various parts of the body, especially the cheeks and the breasts.

61. Living poetry

Do you too remember
when you looked into my eyes and said:
'You're all the beautiful poetry
that I am yet to compose.'

Blazing Flames, Shatavadhani Ganesh, Contemporary, Bengaluru

62. How do you know each other?

On the way to the forest
other women on the road asked Sita:
'Is this handsome man
your husband?'

Her smiling cheeks
embarrassed eyes
and downward glance
answered eloquently for her.

Hanuman's Play

Legend has it that Hanuman inscribed this play on great slabs of stone and threw it into a lake on the banks of the Narmada. It was recovered, much later, by some fishermen in King Bhoja's kingdom.

63. Philosopher's stone

If its magical touch
turns even their flaws
into endearing virtues

like the philosopher's stone
turns all metals into gold

then it's love.

Collection of Prakrit Verse

Prakrit had the brand identity of being the language of love and romance. As one famous Prakrit gaha goes: 'You don't know Prakrit poetry and you dare speak of love? For shame!'

64. Love God on retainer

I'm quite convinced that
the Love God must be on her payroll.
One quick glance from her
and his arrows fly thither.

Treasury of Verse-Jewels, 1000 CE, Bengal

The arch of a beautiful girl's eyebrow is often compared to the Love God's bow.

65. Women's locker room

How lucky
that you remember
every little detail –
how he smiled
how he looked
even how he felt.

As for me
I felt his hand
slide across my waist.
After that
try as I might
I can't remember a damned thing.

Ambrosia for the Ears, 1200 CE, Bengal

This verse is said to be by the Chalukyan Queen Vidya, who announced: 'The famous poet Dandi, not knowing my complexion, foolishly described the goddess Sarasvati as white.'

66. Magical arrow

She's the Love God's own arrow
the latest model
never seen before.

If you're struck
it's difficult to live with the heartbreak.
If you aren't
have you really lived?

Light on Love, 1000 CE, Malwa

The form of this verse is the doha – like the dohas of Kabir.

67. Can't have enough

When he's in front of me
full of sweet nothings
I'm not quite sure:
Have I turned
all eyes
or all ears?

Amaru's Hundred, 600 CE?

The story goes that Adi Shankara was challenged in debate with questions on love. Clueless on these matters as a monk, he entered the body of King Amaru, learnt the syllabus, and not only won the debate but also wrote *Amaru's Hundred* in the process.

68. Perfect as she is

You may see her aplenty
but each time
she dazzles anew.

She has no need for a smile:
her radiance
smiles for her.

She has no need for a drink:
her limbs sway gracefully
all the same.

She has no need for words:
her eyes
do a fine job already.

Mahabharata, Vyasa

This is Vyasa's testament to Draupadi's beauty in the Mahabharata.

69. Words fall short

Her face is like
the moon, yes.
And yes, her lips
are heaven's ambrosia.

But
pulling her close
by the hair
for a kiss
all fire and frenzy –
any figures of speech for that?

Seven Hundred Gahas, 100 CE?, Deccan

70. Rare catch

She's the boss in bed.
Guru in all matters of love.
My personal lucky charm.
When it comes to work
she's efficient as a housekeeper.

When the elders are around –
she's the quintessential good girl.

Seven Hundred Aryas, Govardhana, 1100 CE, Bengal

71. Sound advice

Children, know this:
the husband is to the wife
and the wife to the husband:
lover and friend
the essence of companionship
every desire and every wealth
life itself.

Malati and Madhava, Bhavabhuti, 700 CE, Kanyakubja

72. Spoils of war

Her earrings
sparkling with pearls
look ever so pretty –

like stars
held as prisoners of war
after her face
defeated the moon in its grace.

Sharngadhara's Anthology, 1300 CE, Ranthambore

Sanskrit poetry frequently imagines the moon as a king who rules over the stars.

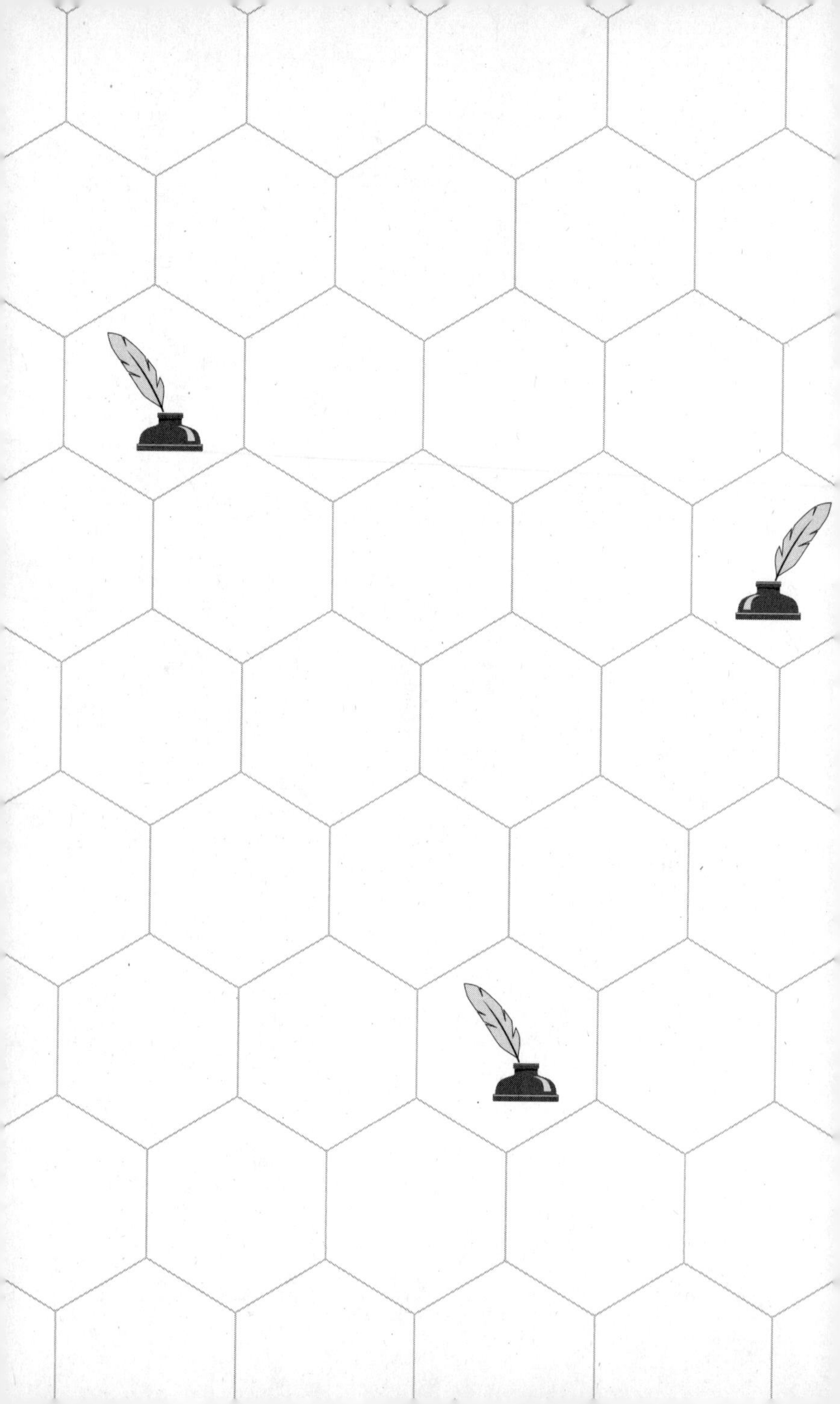

HOW TO YEARN

73. Here there and everywhere

Your curves in the vines
your glance in the deer's startled look
your face in the moon
and your rich tresses in
the peacock's fanned-out feathers.
The arch of your brows in the rising waves –

flashes of you everywhere
driving me to desperation
that I cannot see you whole.

Cloud Messenger, Kalidasa, 400 CE?

Cloud Messenger is the most imitated poem in Indian history. Hundreds of spin-offs have been written in a variety of languages, dispatching a menagerie of animals to various parts of the country. More recent messengers have visited such places as New York and the Mediterranean.

74. I’m no hero

They say that Rama,
parted from Sita,
held back the mighty ocean
to build a bridge.

And here I am,
parted from her –
can’t even
hold back
a few tears.

Vidyakara Mishra’s Thousand, 1800 CE

75. After death do us part

God,

I don't mind dying
and this body
disintegrating
back into the five –

earth to earth
fire to fire
water to water
air to air
space back to space.

But I ask this much of you
with head bowed –

let me be
the water in her well
the light on her mirror
the space in her home
the earth on her path
and
the breeze from her fan.

Line-up of Good Verse, 1400 CE, Kashmir

76. Today doesn't count

God has a rather mean streak
don't you think?
Look how he counts our days.

Even those days
when I've not
snuggled against her at all
(not even for a moment)
he ticks off as a day.

Could he not write it off?

Arrangement of Verses, 1600 CE, Maharashtra

77. Advaita philosophy

It is her at home
her everywhere I turn
her walking ahead
and her right behind
her in my arms in bed
her on every path I tread.

Ill as I am from wanting her
there is nothing in my world
but her
her
her
her
her
her
her.

Not a place without her –
what Advaita is this?

Amaru's Hundred, 600 CE?

Advaita philosophy maintains that there is no duality in the world – there is only one Brahman, and everything else is an illusion.

78. One-upmanship

Those men are fortunate
who are so used to seeing their lovers
that they see them in everything
even when they are far apart.

As for me, my heart
is so engrossed in her alone
that I am left wondering:
Are there even other things in this world
for me to see her in?

Bhartrisarasvata's Anthology, Bhartrisarasvata, 1000 CE, Kashmir

79. Finding distractions

Missing you
I painted on the rocks
you being upset with me
and I tried to paint myself
fallen at your feet, saying sorry
till tears welled up
and all was a blur.

Cruel fate won't even
let us be together
in my little games.

Cloud Messenger, Kalidasa, 400 CE?

80. Letter from a lover

Greetings,

To my darling __________ in town __________, who is more handsome than the Love God himself, who has stolen many hearts with his composure, nobility, and good looks. From __________ in town __________, who always follows every word you say. With all my love, longing, the tightest hugs, and tears, I have something to say –
All is well here. You must keep delighting me with word that you're well. From the day your journey started, I haven't had a moment of peace, burning as I have been from the grief of being parted from you. As the poem goes,

> Darling!
> Where is peace
> for those tormented by separation's fire
> until they can find release
> by plunging into the lake of love
> with its clear waters of pleasure?

Thinking of all this, take pity on me, and though you have a great deal to accomplish there, abandon it all and come here to me, enliven my limbs, scorched in the flames of separation, with the ambrosial sight of you! You mustn't drag your feet.

Guide to Letter Writing, 1500 CE, Gurjara

Guide to Letter Writing is a curious collection of letter templates evidently written as a manual for professional letter writers in Gujarat. It is written in a local Sanskrit with many usages peculiar to that region of Gujarat.

81. Trip down memory lane

It became her stake in our bedroom dice games
a leash around my neck while making love
our fan when we were all sweaty after
her bedspread when we fought and slept apart:

this very shawl that she wore
which fate has now returned to me.

Jasmine Garland, Dhiranaga, 600–1000 CE

Jasmine Garland reimagines the final episode of the Ramayana, concluding the story with Rama and Sita's reunion.

82. To the moon, sky

Friend moon,
you're pale and don't sleep a wink at night
and you're wasting away day after day.
Are you pining away for her
just as I am?

Line-up of Good Verse, 1400 CE, Kashmir

People pining away for their lovers get so thin in Sanskrit love poetry that their bracelets slip off their wrists, falling to the floor.

83. Nobody's fool, but my own

A thakur fallen from grace, a famished brahmin, an immodest young call girl, and a man parted from his lover – all make fools of themselves with sweet daydreams of their unfulfilled longings.

Princess Karpuramanjari, Rajashekhara, 900 CE, Kanyakubja

Princess Karpuramanjari was commissioned for production by the author's very learned wife and Chauhan princess, Avantisundari. Elsewhere, he repeatedly cites her opinions on various aspects of literary theory.

84. Miles to go before we meet

Back then
holding you close
I wouldn't even wear a necklace
lest it get in the way.

And today
rivers
mountains
and oceans
stand between us.

Ambrosia for the Ears, 1200 CE, Bengal

Rama says this while separated from Sita.

85. Loving from a distance

Fly, O wind!
Touch Sita
then touch me again.
In you, I'll find her caress
and our eyes will meet
in the moon.

Ramayana, Valmiki

Rama, known best for being prim and proper, is actually very romantic in the Ramayana. His laments when Sita is kidnapped can make anyone misty-eyed.

86. Global warming

Darling! I think it's best that
you put off your flight a bit.
The weather here is … rather odd.
Even the moonbeams feel
searingly hot.

Ambrosia for the Ears, 1200 CE, Bengal

In Sanskrit poetry, cool, romantic moonlit nights feel unbearably hot to lovers away from each other. Everything that conjures up a romantic mood – cooing koels, spring flowers, moonlight – turns into a source of agony when the lover is not around.

87. Just maybe

These cool Himalayan winds
that burst open
the tender shoots of the deodar
and drink the fragrance of its sap
hurry southwards to me.

I embrace them, my love
for what if
by the tiniest chance
they had touched you?

Cloud Messenger, Kalidasa, 400 CE?

The deodar tree has a spicy, woody scent that imparts a delicious fragrance to the air around it. It is the central note in many popular perfumes.

88. Walking, talking inscription

As you sit thinking of him
your palms pressed hard
into your cheeks
tinging them coppery red
your fingers etching lines –

it seems you are inscribing
a plaque commemorating
the good fortune
of some lucky, lucky man.

Bhartrisarasvata's Anthology, Bhartrisarasvata, 1000 CE, Kashmir

89. Ready to mingle

When your girlfriend
is next to you
moonlit nights
cool and breezy
just seem to fly by.

When your girlfriend
is far away
the same moonlit nights
burn you up.

As for me
there is no girlfriend
neither beside me
nor far away

the moon
is just the moon
a shiny mirror in the sky
in usual thermodynamic equilibrium.

Wishing Stone of Stories, Merutunga, 1300 CE, Gurjara

The story goes that this was composed by Kulachandra, who was King Bhoja's general. Hearing this sad confession, Bhoja 'gifted' him a beautiful girl.

90. Daren't risk it

He's far away on work.

Longing to see him
she sketches him on the wall:
his head, shoulders and arms
but not his legs –

can't risk him going away again.

Vidyakara Mishra's Thousand, 1800 CE

The work brings together about a thousand verses on eclectic topics, largely written by poets from Mithila.

91. Falling prey to love

This dratted God of love
torments my heart
like a hunter does a deer –

first mesmerizing me with the music
of the tinkling bells of her waistband

then dazing me
with the blinding torch
of passion

then ensnaring me
in her eyes
and shooting his arrows
one after another

and now he barbeques me
in the fire of my pain
at being parted from her.

Wedding of Subhadra, Sudhindra Tirtha, 1600 CE, Karnata

These were the old tricks used by hunters – attracting deer with music, and blinding them with powerful lanterns before capturing them. Sudhindra Tirtha was the guru of the well-known saint Raghavendra Swami of Mantralaya.

92. Consoling yourself

As I thirst for her
this is no small comfort
this is what gives me life:

just knowing that
her feet and mine
still tread the one same earth.

Ramayana, Valmiki

93. The great Indian pot trick

If somehow
I get to
meet him again
you'll see something
none has seen before:

how I'll meld into him
limb into limb
like water
into a parched clay pot.

Apabhramsha Grammar, 1100 CE, Gurjara

This is neither Sanskrit nor Prakrit, but Apabhramsha – the stage of language that immediately preceded today's north Indian languages.

94. Daydreams

When my luck turns
and I see her again
I can't decide –

Shall I be like Vishnu
and set her down firmly
in my heart?

Or shall I be like Shiva
and fuse her body with mine?

Arrangement of Verses, 1600 CE, Maharashtra

Vishnu carries Lakshmi on his chest, and Shiva unites with Parvati in a single body as Ardhanarishvara.

95. How are you doing today?

Like a practised potter
fate squeezes my heart
into a lump of clay
and plops it
on to the wheel of worry
driving it
round and round
faster and faster
smacking me with new miseries.
What is he trying to make?
I'm not quite sure.

Line-up of Good Verse, 1400 CE, Kashmir

When this verse is read aloud, repeating sequences of light and heavy syllables in the poetic metre give the illusion of a spinning wheel.

96. Man proposes, God disposes

Everything that
my poor mind writes
with its chalk of hope
on the board of my heart

fate
like a little boy
laughs to itself
and wipes away.

Seven Hundred Gahas, 100 CE?, Deccan

97. Love moves in mysterious ways

To hear he's hurting
from being away
brings joy

but that joy
brings more hurt
(that he's away)

I tell you
love is weird.

Collection of Prakrit Verse

98. First day is hardest

He just left today
and already today
they've become empty –

the streets
the temples
the crossings

and my heart.

Seven Hundred Gahas, 100 CE?, Deccan

99. Multiplication

A river's flood
gushes forth
in a hundred streams
when it comes up against
rocks that break its pace

and love too
does just that
as it negotiates
the hurdles to
being together.

Urvashi Won by Valour, Kalidasa, 400 CE?

100. Post-breakup intel

‘Is she well?’
        ‘She lives.’
‘I asked if she’s well.’
        ‘And I said she’s alive.’
‘Why do you say that over and over?’
        ‘Am I to declare her dead
        while she manages to breathe…’

Ambrosia for the Ears, 1200 CE, Bengal

101. Only heartache

When you're away
my heart aches from missing you.
When you're here
my heart aches
at the prospect of missing you.
Either way
I only know heartache.

Line-up of Good Verse, 1400 CE, Kashmir

102. Fanning the flames

Friends,
stop fanning me
with the lotus leaf.
The breeze only fans my heart's fire –
it's no relief.

Line-up of Good Verse, 1400 CE, Kashmir

103. Finding excuses

Even when we hung out with friends
and I was telling you
things that I could well say out loud
I leaned in to whisper
because I couldn't resist
brushing my lips
against your cheek.

Cloud Messenger, Kalidasa, 400 CE?

104. Lies, damned lies and poetry

This time, I'm not
sending him a poem
that says I miss him.
He might brush it off
as a poet's hyperbole.

Instead, take to him
these earrings of mine
where the kohl from my eyes
flowing freely with my tears
has already
inked for him
a message.

Ambrosia for the Ears, 1200 CE, Bengal

105. Not a rationalist

'Don't die of heartbreak.
You can see him again
but only if you live,' you say?

I hear you, friends.
But we're discussing love here
not rationality.

Seven Hundred Gahas, 100 CE?, Deccan

106. I'm proud of me

Without seeing your lovely face
without drinking in your words
without being by your side
I managed to live, just a little –
such is my boast.

Without resting my head
on the pillow of your arm
without losing myself
in the night of your hair
without nestling
playfully in your lap
I managed to sleep, just a little –
such is my boast.

Balram Shukla, Contemporary, New Delhi

107. Love hangover

The greater the joys you find in making love
the more intolerable being away becomes –
the more delectable the feast
the worse it feels when you throw up.

Seven Hundred Gahas, 100 CE?, Deccan

107. I prefer long distance

Be with her
or be away from her?

I'd rather be away.

When I'm with her
I see her there,
when I'm away
I see her everywhere.

Ambrosia for the Ears, 1200 CE, Bengal

109. Missing her

If she were but a pond
her eyes two lilies
her face a lotus
her slender arms lotus stalks
her dancing eyebrows ripples
I would plunge at once
into the cool waters of her loveliness
and be rid of this searing pain
that threatens to rip life from limb.

Treasury of Verse-Jewels, 1000 CE, Bengal

Jawaharlal Nehru showed a personal interest in the *Treasury of Verse-Jewels* and had a manuscript acquired from Nepal so it could be published.

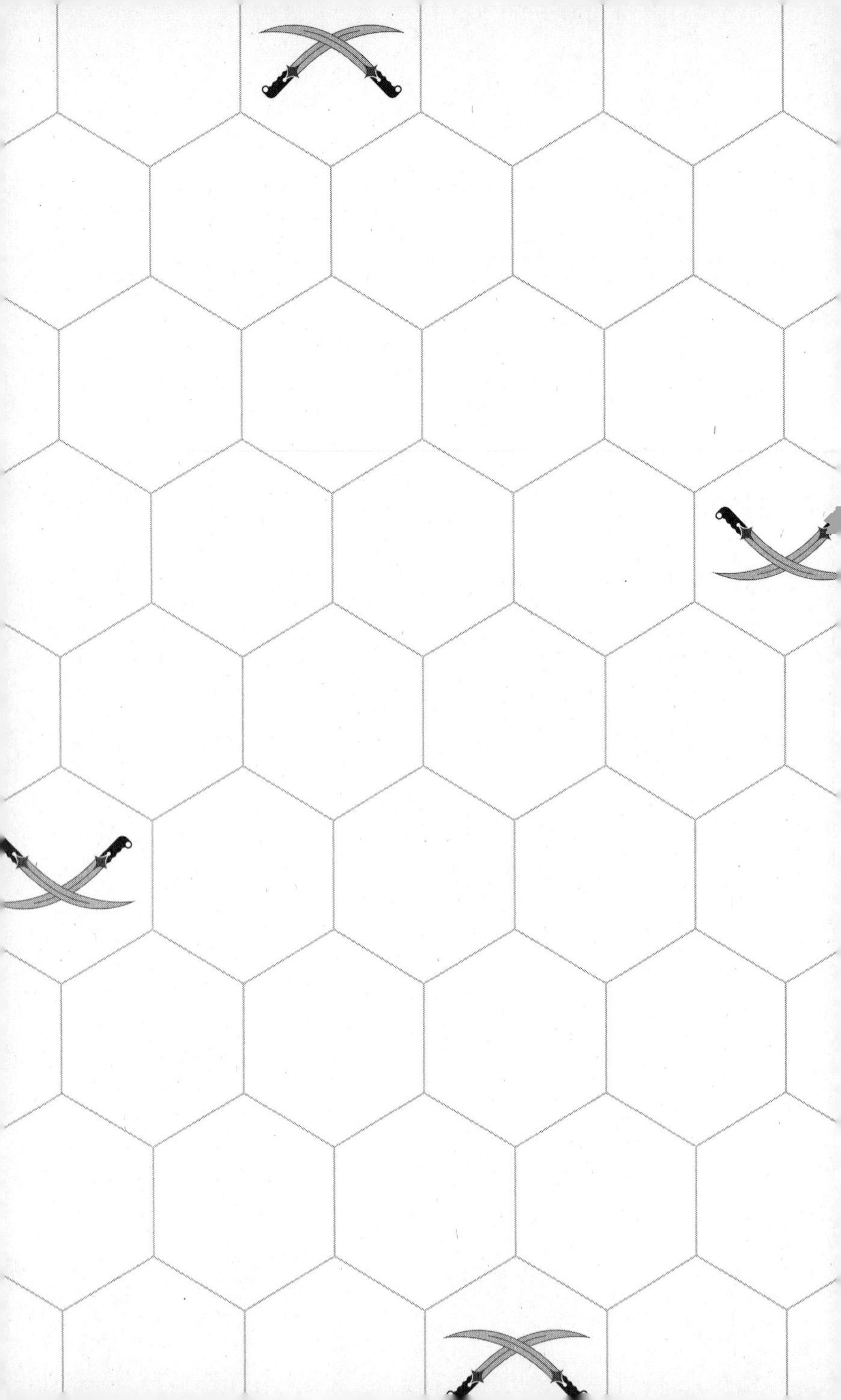

HOW TO QUARREL

110. Pick a fight today

Love seems to have dulled?
Just go give it a good polish
on that whetstone
called the lover's tiff.

Princess Lilavai, Kouhala, 800 CE

111. Confidence

Dear God,
make him hang out
with other women more.
He does not seem to realize
what a catch I am.

Seven Hundred Gahas, 100 CE?, Deccan

112. Outlier

The creator gave you
eyes like lilies
a face like a lotus
teeth like jasmine
lips like fresh buds
limbs tender like champaka blossoms.
Why then, darling
a heart like stone?

Light on Ten Kinds of Drama

Light on Ten Kinds of Drama is a commentary on Dhananjaya's *Ten Kinds of Drama*, which discusses several strategies for cajoling a cross lover. This verse is an example of the first strategy: sweet talk. Others include giving gifts, winning over her friends, falling at her feet, pretending indifference, and engineering a distraction.

113. Two negatives make a positive

Upset with him
she resolutely
turned the other way
and fell asleep

and in her dream
again upset
she resolutely
turned the other way

and found herself
back to square one.

Seven Hundred Gahas, 100 CE?, Deccan

114. Wingwoman to the rescue

What? You're letting him off
with just a sorry?
He deserves no less than
rigorous imprisonment
in your arms.

Treasury of Verse-Jewels, 1000 CE, Bengal

115. Taking no chances

I still remember it like yesterday –
that stony silence after a fight
broken by my sneeze.

She bit her lip
holding back a 'bless you'
but still touched
her auspicious gold earring
to ward off bad luck.

Thief's Fifty, Bilhana, 1000 CE, Kashmir

Legend has it that the *Thief's Fifty* was composed by Bilhana in prison while he awaited death for daring to romance a princess.

116. I'm taking my stuff

If you're angry with me, love
I wouldn't dream
of changing your mind.

Before I move out –
you have to return
with interest
every single hug
and every single kiss.

Treasury of Verse-Jewels, 1000 CE, Bengal

Staking hugs and kisses in dice games was a favourite pastime of lovers.

117. Letter from the angry husband

Greetings,

From _________ in _________ town, who duly conveys his well-being as follows to his wife _________ in town _________.

I am well here. Please dispatch a message informing me that everybody there is well.

Another matter: every single person who comes from the town – every single one – comes bearing complaints about our home. Nothing seems to get done there if I am not present for every little thing. I left you a couple of months' worth of groceries, but you blew through it in all of eighteen days. You burn me at every step. But it's not your fault. This is my own fault, for I must have made some horrible mistake in another life. After all, they say:

> The knowledge you teach
> the wealth you share
> the daughter you give in marriage
> you get back
> as good as you give
> in life after life.

Also: No matter how many times I tell you to do something, you go and do exactly the opposite. What's the point of going on and on? I will just say this – behave in a way that befits your family's standing.

Guide to Letter Writing, 1500 CE, Gurjara

118. Hard-hearted

The night is nearly extinguished
and the moon grows gaunt.
The lamp by our bed
is nodding off, half asleep.
I have admitted defeat
but still you fume…

Did your heart grow so firm
taking lessons from your breasts?

Wishing Stone of Stories, Merutunga, 1300 CE, Gurjara

The story goes that the poet, Mayura, said the first few lines to his wife. Then a voice from outside piped up, supplying the punchline. It was Bana, the famed author of the *Kadambari*, who was within earshot.

119. Don't marry an academic

The break is done
and the semester is here
stealing his attention
like a second wife.
His lectures are all
that he can think about.
I can flirt all I like –
I'm not getting any tonight.

Wishing Tree of Rasa, 1700 CE

120. Cold war

They've had a tiff –

both pretend
to be asleep
both unyielding
both listening intently
for a sound from the other
both absolutely still
refusing even to breathe aloud.

Who will break first?

Seven Hundred Gahas, 100 CE?, Deccan

121. Feat of strength

Flinging my hand aside
you set off with easy stride.
But that's no mighty feat.
Leave my heart, if you can
then I'll admit defeat.

Line-up of Good Verse, 1400 CE, Kashmir

122. Passive-aggressive

Enough apologies, dear
please leave.
You haven't made
even a fraction
of a mistake.
It's my own fate
that frowns on me.

But don't worry
I won't suffer long.
If your love for me
once so unshakeable
is now no more
my life – so much more fragile –
will not take long to follow.

Amaru's Hundred, 600 CE?

123. Lucky escape

After a fight
the husband fell
at his angry wife's feet.
Their toddler
giggling at the game
climbed on his back
and her anger vanished
in a burst of laughter.

Seven Hundred Gahas, 100 CE?, Deccan

124. Dry and unfeeling

Give her your heart.

I know it is
dry and unfeeling
like a pile of wood

but she's at death's door
pining away for your love.

(We could always use it
for her funeral pyre.)

Ambrosia for the Ears, 1200 CE, Bengal

125. How the fire starts

It fumes in her heart
flares into her gestures
simmers in her body
blazes in her eyes
erupts on her face
and spurts out as words –
anger, when she's been
slighted by her lover.

Ambrosia for the Ears, 1200 CE, Bengal

126. Kiss and make up

As he drank from her lips
the flush of anger
slowly drained from her face
like wine
from a crystal goblet.

Slaying of the King of Gauda, Vakpatiraja, 700 CE, Kanyakubja

127. Barefaced lies

Your actions hurt
but what hurts more
are your barefaced lies.

A cut hurts
but the sting of a needle
is far worse.

Seven Hundred Aryas, Govardhana, 1100 CE, Bengal

128. Not fooling anyone

Oh you're here.
You must have fought with her
or did she kick you to the curb?
After all, I'm the pavilion you return to
when you're booted out of the dating game.
Why incite my hopeless, despairing heart?
No point giving you bitter medicine.
Nice to see you. Now scram.

The Lotus Gift, Shudraka

129. Planning to sulk

He shall come back from his travels.

I shall sulk at him
(just for the fun of it).

He shall indulge me
with sweet nothings.

Only a few lucky folks
have this chain of daydreams
come true.

Seven Hundred Gahas, 100 CE?, Deccan

HOW TO MAKE LOVE

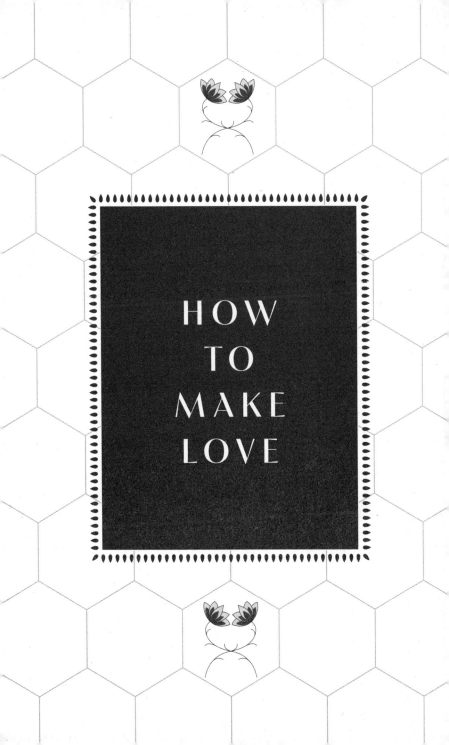

130. BDSM

If impassioned women don't
rough you up, dragging you by the hair
if they don't tie you up with their girdle-strings
and strike you with flowers
do you even deserve to be called a lover?

If women toy with you in bed
quite shamelessly
like you're their slave
love favours you, you lucky dog
and your youth is one grand party.

The Kick, Shyamilaka

The Kick pokes fun at a sanctimonious man who enjoys himself with a courtesan but is affronted when she playfully kicks him.

131. Mind over matter

The mighty God of love
just glances their way
and in their passion

the hidden thicket – castleizes
pitch darkness – chandelierizes
the bare ground – mattressizes
even a rock – pillowizes
and plain old dirt – makeupizes.

Warehouse of Verses, 1800 CE

Sanskrit has ways of turning any noun into a verb, which we have tried to replicate in English.

132. Not shy in the sheets

Come night
she calls out a hundred demands
her face lighting up in pleasure.
Come morning
she has face bowed
not even looking me in the eye –
is it really her?

Seven Hundred Gahas, 100 CE?, Deccan

133. The weaker sex

She goes to meet him
in the dead of night
braving the rain
charging through the thorns
crossing a river or two
even stomping on snakes
without a care.

Then she reaches his bed
and pauses for his arm
to help her up.

Vidyakara Mishra's Thousand, 1800 CE

A recurring character in Sanskrit is the Abhisarika, a woman who sneaks out to meet her lover using every trick in the book to avoid being seen.

134. Naturally gifted

It was their first night.
She was such a natural
that he couldn't help but wonder…

Seeing it on his face
she sketched something on the wall:

a lion cub
half emerging just then
from his mother's womb
already pouncing at an elephant
with natural flair.

He got his answer
and smiled.

Allegorical Pearls, 1700 CE

135. First night

Close embraces were had
feisty kisses were given
clothes were discarded

and our first night
was already over

(even before the main course could begin).

Light on Love, 1000 CE, Malwa

136. Better than the first night

Our first night together
was divine. But even better –
seeing her cheeks flush red
the next morning
as the night came flooding back.

Seven Hundred Gahas, 100 CE?, Deccan

137. Next morning

She was so embarrassed
they had to coax her into
the honeymoon suite.

And in the morning
when they called her
she put her phone on silent.

Seven Hundred Aryas, Govardhana, 1100 CE, Bengal

We have slightly modernized the context of the verse.

138. Morning after

How glorious is a woman's face
at the start of the night
hair done up
make-up chosen with the greatest care.
And how much more gorgeous –
make-up smudged, hair tousled
the morning after?

Princess Lilavai, Kouhala, 800 CE

139. Some guys have all the luck

When I look at her
I envy Indra's thousand eyes
when I kiss her
I envy Adishesha's thousand tongues
and when I hug her
I envy Kartaviryarjuna's thousand arms.

Ambrosial Ocean of Verse, 1300 CE, Karnata

Kartaviryarjuna, the king of Mahishmati, had a thousand arms. Adishesha, the serpent that carries the world on his hood, has a thousand heads.

140. Never too much

You've kissed her a hundred times
but kiss her again.
You've hugged him a thousand times
but hug him again.
You have made love, of course
but do it again.
Only in love
is excess a virtue.

Light on Suggestion, 800 CE, Kashmir

141. What are you doing tonight?

The sun slips into the sea

and the bee, drunk on honey
stumbles into the lotus bud.

The birds retreat
into the hollows of trees

as desire steals its way
into the hearts of women.

Tales of Bhoja, 1500 CE?

The story goes that this verse was a collaborative effort by the great poets of Bhoja's court. Each poet contributed a line, and Kalidasa topped it off with the final bit.

142. Climax

Sweat trickled
from the orb of the moon.
Darkness, bound by flowers
had come untangled.
Just a moment ago
buds of white ketaki flowers
blossomed in a joyous smile.
The dance of the earrings stilled.
Both dark lilies rolled shut.
A final gasp
and the red coral quietened.
Beyond this,
I know not what happened.

Tales of Bhoja, 1500 CE?

There is a genre of verses that uses symbols to describe what happens at the 'end of lovemaking'. Legend says this was Kalidasa's winning poem in a contest with Bhavabhuti.

143. Why study the *Kamasutra*?

What can a monkey
do with a coconut?
(Nothing, unless it knows
how to get to its kernel.)

Similarly
if one doesn't know women –
what they're like
their temperament
what they're good at
where they're from
what they feel
what they do
what they mean when they do what they do

– a clueless man
unskilled in the art of love
messes up
even if he finds a girlfriend.

Secrets of Pleasure, Kokkoka, 800 CE

144. Throw away the textbooks

The *Kamasutra* and such
only have something to say
until your appetite is whet.

Once the wheel of pleasure
begins to spin
there is no textbook
there is no order.

Kamasutra, Mallanaga Vatsyayana

These are the most famous lines of the *Kamasutra*.

145. Role reversal 1

‘Today,’ he said,
‘I’ll be the woman
and you be the man.’

‘No way,’ she demurred,
shaking her head resolutely
but quickly
slipped off her bangles
from her hand
to his.

Ambrosial Ocean of Verse, 1300 CE, Karnata

146. Role reversal 2

After sweet nothings
and sexy commands
when she was done
riding me

blushing a bit
she went to change
and wore my tee by mistake.

So I wore hers.

She saw me
grinned
and said,
'This is much better.'

That, I'll never forget.

Pearl Necklace of Verses, 1200 CE, Deccan

147. No holds barred

Nothing was off limits
nothing was unspeakable
nothing was questionable
nothing was confidential
nothing was too much
as the two fell on each other
wildly, like they were in battle.

Bawd's Counsel, Damodaragupta, 800 CE, Kashmir

148. No restraints

Restraint?
Out the window.
Embarrassment?
They knew no such thing.
Thinking?
No time for it.
That was what their sex was like.

Ambrosial Ocean of Verse, 1300 CE, Karnata

149. Shy but willing

Each part of me
that he studies
I conceal from his gaze
even as I want him
to go on looking.

Seven Hundred Gahas, 100 CE?, Deccan

150. No time to waste

He was embarrassed
as I laughed
and drew him close

when he fumbled
for the hook
and found it already undone.

Seven Hundred Gahas, 100 CE?, Deccan

151. Cowgirl

The tinkling girdle
mingles with low moans
as her hips sway
savouring the pleasure
of being on top –

pearls clatter
as her hair comes undone
in ardour –

breasts rise
as her breath hitches –

lucky is the man whom
a willing woman rides.

Line-up of Good Verse, 1400 CE, Kashmir

152. Moonlit frenzy

It was the moonlit night
that deepened their frenzy.
Or was it their frenzy
that heightened the moonlit night?
Or did both conspire
to inflame their passion?
Or was it their passion
that raised both
to a high crescendo?

Slaying of Ravana, Pravarasena, 500 CE?

153. Caveat amator

Having sex on the first date, especially with a charming girl who's not yet herself in your company, is a risky gamble, much like throwing yourself into a lake of unknown depth.

Rogue and Rake Confer, Ishvaradatta, 400 CE?

Rogue and Rake Confer is one of a set of four plays that paint a very colourful picture of urban life in early India. The streets jostle with princes, poets, grammarians, courtesans, merchants and even a person of the third gender (tritiya prakriti).

154. Quickie

Trembling in the heat
of secret lovemaking
she urges him on,
'My love, hurry!'

That's all it takes.
He's hers now.
She has set his price
and bought him too.

Rogue and Rake Confer, Ishvaradatta, 400 CE?

155. No thanks, heaven

The slow days that men spend with their friends, plotting ideas to get back into the good books of upset lovers: are such days possible in heaven where jealousy does not exist? And the joyful sleep that comes with a woman lying on your chest, her limbs radiating love, her mouth scented with sweet, flowery fragrance: how is that possible in heaven where no one sleeps? And those endearing things she says in shy, sweet, slurred words after she's had a drink or two: how do you hear those in heaven where there is no drinking? How can you make love with your newly-wed, replete with sharp intakes of breath, moans, and so many embraces? Also, let me tell you, I'd more readily bed a doddering old Vedic pandit than an apsara. Apsaras seem to have been living since forever, speak pretentious Sanskrit, and carry intimidating power. They gave birth to holy sages like Vasishtha and Agastya: which man can be himself in their company?

Rogue and Rake Confer, Ishvaradatta, 400 CE?

156. Paradise found

Dazzling jasmine blossoms
in her hair
saffron mingling with sandal
on her limbs
she, lying languidly
on my chest –
this is heaven.
What's up there
are just some leftover crumbs.

Bhartrihari's Three Hundred, Bhartrihari, 300 CE?

157. Pillow talk

Indiscernible murmurs
many tender assurances
some old fights resurfacing
then again, some sly compliments
once more, words dripping with love
trembling voices
more empty promises, some chidings, still more biddings
tinged with sweetness.

Their pillow talk went on and on –
no end in sight.

Ascent of King Kapphina, Shivasvami, 800 CE, Kashmir

158. All-nighter

Lovemaking was at its end
but for one last embrace

make-up had rubbed away
but for perfume's lingering trace

the Love God's arsenal was spent
but for his empty arrow-case

as the night ebbed away
leaving dawn in its place.

Enlivener of Connoisseurs, 1600 CE, Mithila

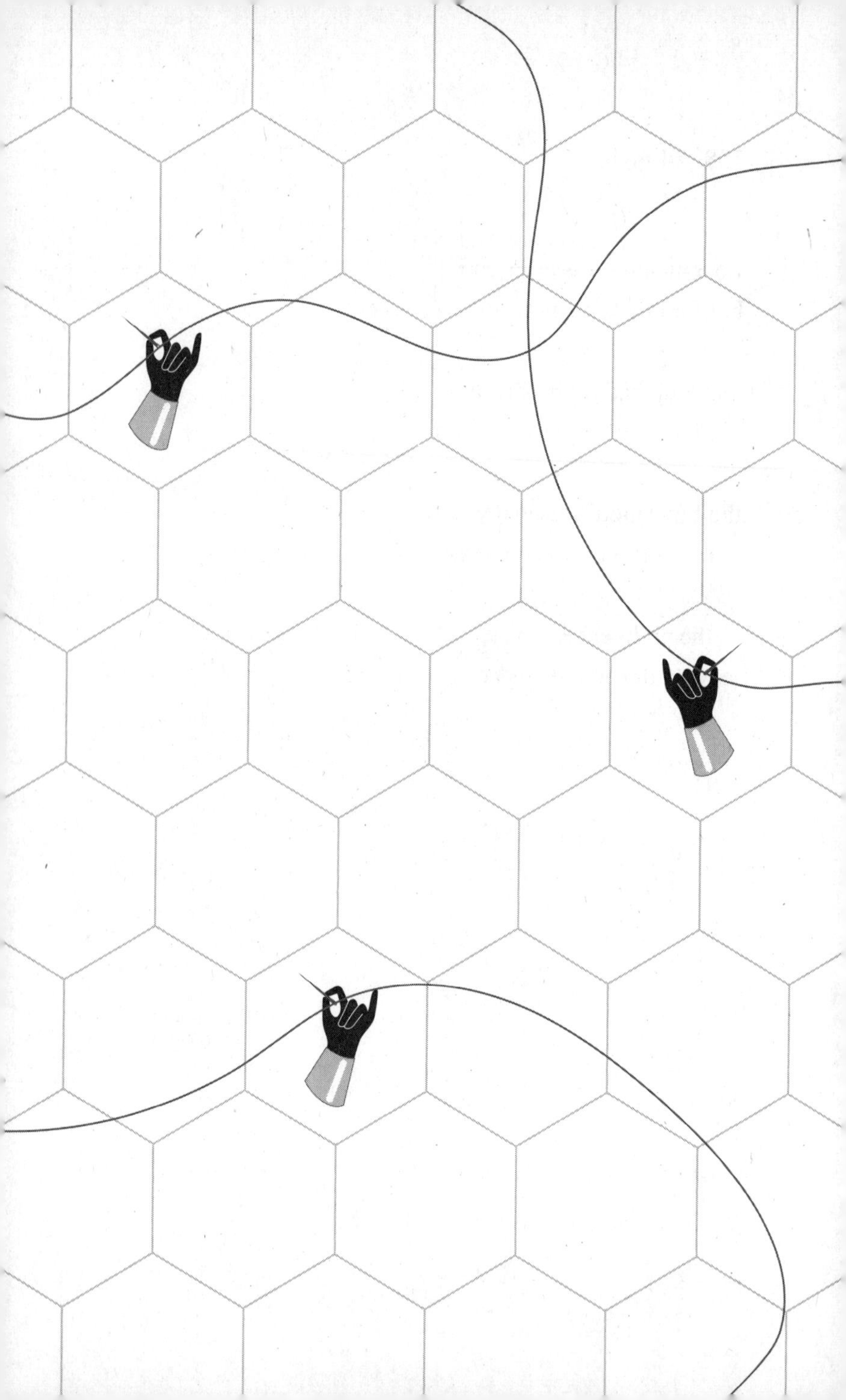

HOW TO MAKE IT WORK

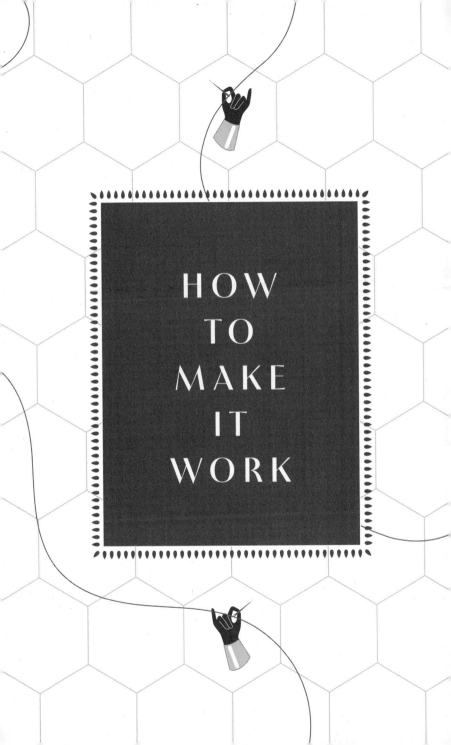

159. Crime and punishment

What should the punishment be
for the crime of being blind to the charms
of poetry, music and love?
The crime is its own punishment.

Seven Hundred Gahas, 100 CE?, Deccan

160. Don't be a tinman

The elephant is held by a tying post
and the horse by the reins.
A woman though
is held by the heart –
if you have it not
goodbye.

Little Clay Cart, Shudraka

The *Little Clay Cart* is the only non-satirical Sanskrit drama to feature a courtesan as the leading character. And in case you were wondering, this is the drama that the Bollywood movie *Utsav*, directed by Girish Karnad, was based on.

161. Don't love a book lover

Dear book,
whose pages
his nails lovingly mark,

You are my
sworn enemy for life.

This beastly man
doesn't give a hoot about me
absorbed as he is in you.

Bundle on Love, 1600 CE?

Marking the lover with one's nails was almost an art in India.

162. Back to square one

Love makes
a fine fool of me
now that it settles
upon him yet again

like a crow at sea
that leaves the ship's mast
and circles the skies
only to return to its old perch.

Vajjalagga

The *Vajjalagga* is a brilliant collection of Prakrit verse compiled by a certain Jayavallabha, about whom we know nothing except his name.

163. Sharing is caring

The deer knows
the doe is thirsty.
The doe knows
the deer is thirsty.

They chance upon a little puddle
with just a splash of water.

Each only pretends
to sip,
eyes lovingly
on the other.

Wishing Tree of Rasa, 1700 CE

The *Wishing Tree of Rasa* also contains six Sanskrit verses written by Aurangzeb's uncle, Shaista Khan.

164. The old ball and chain

Is she politely Victorian
when they've fought?
Does she call him darling
under usual circumstances?
Does she boss him about
when particularly pleased?

Now that's a good marriage.
In all other cases
he's a goat
and she's the rope.

Seven Hundred Aryas, Govardhana, 1100 CE, Bengal

165. Love with a capital L

If you let their slips pass
if you peer into *Vogue* for advice
if you can bear to be apart
whatever it is –
it is not Love.

Treasury of Gahas, 1000 CE

The *Kamasutra* even has a section on how women must respond to their lovers' slips: 'a great big fight with much sobbing, anguish, tossing of hair…' We have modernized the context of the verse.

166. Every teenager

I want to ask her out
but what might she say?
It's killing me.
And I want to go for it.
And I'm terrified.

Wedding of Kadambari, Narasimha, 1300 CE, Andhra

167. Don't hold back

If you let water flow
as it likes
it charts its own
orderly course.

But if you dam it up
and the walls shatter
all hell breaks loose.

When love strikes one
who is used to
the pleasures of life
it makes itself felt
one step at a time.

But if it finds someone
who has always held back –
what happens then?
Pure mayhem.

Kusha and Kumudvati, Atiratrayajva, 1600 CE, Dravida

Kusha and Kumudvati presents the romance of Rama's son Kusha and princess Kumudvati. Atiratrayajva was the younger brother of the famous poet and prime minister at the Madurai court, Nilakantha Dikshita.

168. Upanishad of marriage

Already the next morning
the shehnai and dazzling lights
will seem like distant memories.
State coffers will swallow their share
of the gold and gems.
Money may invite trouble.
The wedding finery will crumble to dust.

What stands you both in good stead
are the virtues you embody –
this is the Upanishad of good marriage.

Handful of Thorns, Krishna S. Arjunwadkar, 1926–2013, Pune

Handful of Thorns satirizes classical poets while examining modern life from a variety of perspectives. Full of humour and biting sarcasm, it is perhaps the most enjoyable modern Sanskrit work.

169. Let me count the ways

There are many kinds of passion:

The golden one endures fire, friction and pliers without losing its sheen. The copper one stays pure, but you must make the effort to keep polishing it or it'll become dull. As for the brass – you can lovingly oil it as much as you like, but it'll still get dirty. Leaden passion will forever be dull – at the start, in the middle, and at the end. The iron passion is sharp, hard and unbending. The jewelled passion is transparent, immaculate, and unchanging. As for the glassy passion – it is brittle and looks out for betrayal. And the stony passion has gravitas, but it is dry and heartless.

Ways of the Madam, Kshemendra, 1000 CE, Kashmir

Kshemendra was a Kashmiri satirist. Some of his favourite targets were bureaucrats, astrologers, and foreign students from Bengal.

170. All for you

If the sky were paper, the ocean an inkpot, Brahma himself the scribe, and thousand-tongued Vasuki the orator, her suffering for you might somehow be described, with a lot of difficulty, but only if you had a few thousand aeons to spare.

Princess Vasavadatta, Subandhu, 500 CE?

Princess Vasavadatta is famous for inaugurating the era of punning in Sanskrit. Subandhu playfully claims that every letter he writes is punned.

171. Doing things together

If they
like a pair of eyes
stay up together
fall asleep together
if they rejoice together
and weep together
those lucky ones
have found true love,
love that lasts a lifetime.

Mallikamakaranda, Ramachandra, 1100 CE, Gurjara

Ramachandra was a Jain monk and the prolific author of a hundred books. We hear that the Chalukyan king Ajayapala tortured him to death by placing him on a hot copper plate.

172. Self-goal

Her husband is very possessive.
He does not let her go out at night
to pick the mahua blossoms.

Simple-minded as he is
he leaves the house at night
to pick the blossoms himself.

Seven Hundred Gahas, 100 CE?, Deccan

The mahua tree blossoms at night and the flowers fall to the ground by dawn.

173. Taking out the trash

Deceiving love
forced love
love that smells money
love based on compliance –
Godspeed to them all.

Seven Hundred Gahas, 100 CE?, Deccan

174. Enemies begone

I dig up this plant
most powerful of all
that fends off a rival wife
and wins me my husband.

O plant with outstretched leaves!
O bringer of good fortune!
One impelled by the gods!
Overpowering one!
Blow my rival away
make my husband just my own.

Husband!
I place this conquering plant
by you
I have harnessed you
with this greatly victorious plant.
May your heart speedily
follow me
like a cow its calf
like water
flowing down a path.

Rig Veda, Indrani

This Rig Vedic hymn for banishing rivals in love is attributed to Indrani, the wife of Indra. Inquiries about the identity of the plant will not be entertained.

175. Is it love?

If you aren't staying up nights
if you aren't even a teeny bit jealous
if you don't get upset at anything they do
if you don't sulk even a bit
if you don't give each other
sweet compliments

there's no love there.

Seven Hundred Gahas, 100 CE?, Deccan

176. Not worth salvaging

When they don't care enough
to even be angry
when affection has broken down
and even goodwill is dead –

if you're still begging for love
what kind of love is it anyway?

Vajjalagga

177. Beyond repair

Once you break up
seeing that it was all a lie
it can never be the same
even if you get back together.

Once you've boiled water
you can cool it all you want
but it'll never taste the same.

Seven Hundred Gahas, 100 CE?, Deccan

178. Frenzied love

When women pour themselves into something
with the fervour of frenzied love
even God squirms
to throw a wrench in the works.

Bhartrihari's Three Hundred, 300 CE?

179. Message to her friends

You are her friends
and I'll tell you this much:
she is my everything.

When I'm away
her life flickers
like a flame in the wind
and without her
my life is plunged
into darkness.

Take good care of her.

Pearl Necklace of Verses, 1200 CE, Deccan

180. Love that sticks

Don’t let love into your heart.

But if you do
be like wool that’s dyed red.

You can wash it all you like
but it won’t let go of its colour
and take on another.

Munichandra’s Gaha Treasury

Red manjistha dye binds wonderfully well to wool, providing a permanent and unfading colour.

181. Don't care for your opinion

I'm a simple village girl –
none of those airs and graces
you'll find in me.
Those hoity-toity city girls –
I steal their husbands.

Say what you will
I am what I am.

Seven Hundred Gahas, 100 CE?, Deccan

182. A bad date

The first hour was wasted
on stories of his favourite sports.
The next quarter went by
with him offering me toffees.
Then he spent another hour
droning on about his gym routine.
And after that –
trust me, you don't want to know.

The Kick, Shyamilaka

183. Afraid to burn

Like logs of wood
too damp to light up in a blaze
the hearts of those
who are easily embarrassed
when inflamed by passion
crackle and simmer from within.

Light on Love, 1000 CE, Malwa

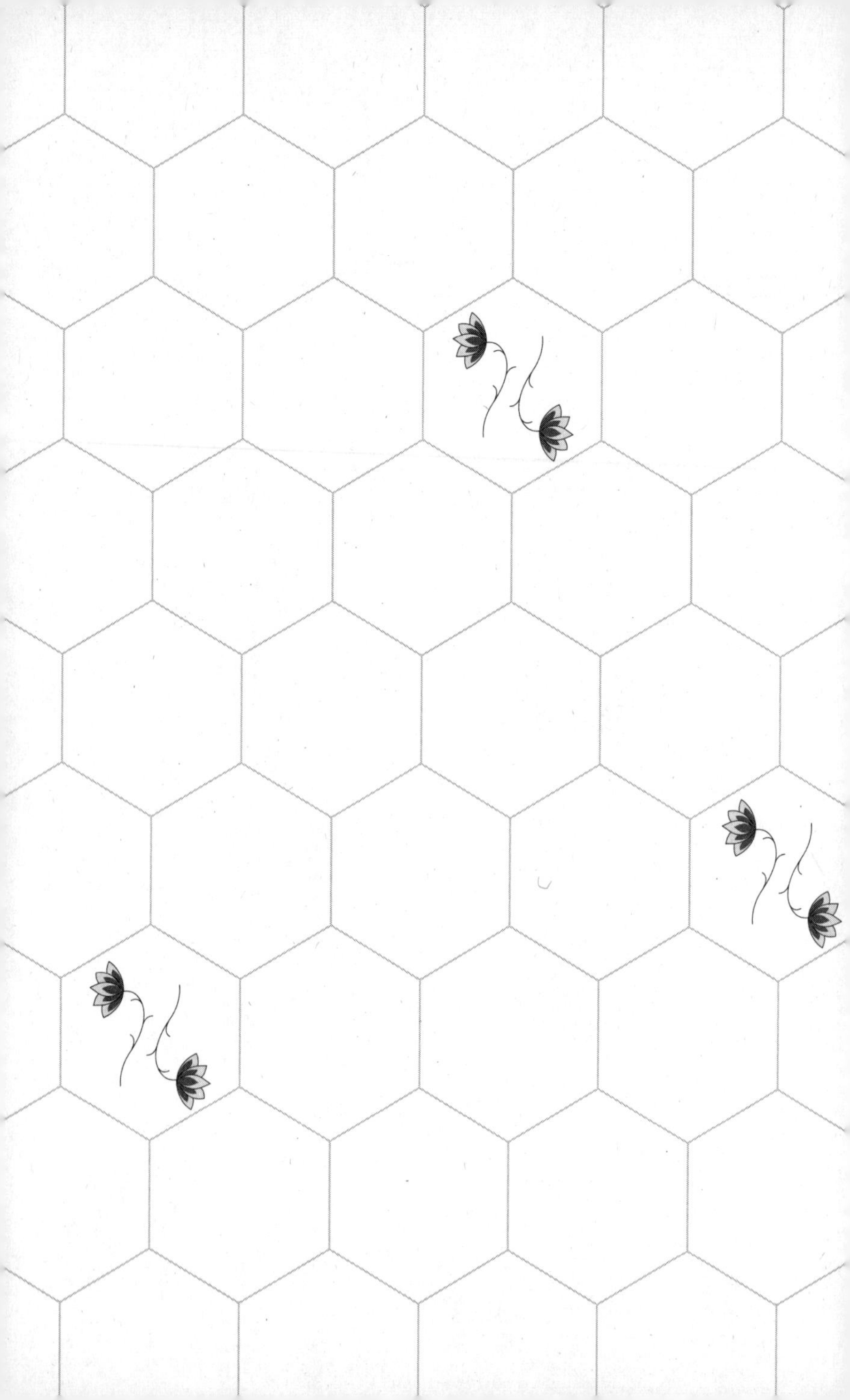

HOW TO BREAK UP

184. Forgive you for what?

Sure, I'll forgive you.
Just tell me what I should forgive:
What you did?
What you're doing?
Or what you'll do next?

Seven Hundred Gahas, 100 CE?, Deccan

This is said to have been composed by Reva, one of the handful of female Prakrit poets featured in *Seven Hundred Gahas*. Some others are Roha, Mahavi, Anulacchi, Vaddavahi and Sasippaha. Nothing more is known about them.

185. There's always a hitch

He's easy on the eyes (like the moon)
voice is rich (like a koel in spring)
amazing kisser (gentle as a dove)
walks with gravitas (graceful as a swan)
wild in bed (like an untamed elephant)
it's everything a woman could want.
It would all be perfect
if not for one little snag:
he's my husband.

Line-up of Good Verse, 1400 CE, Kashmir

186. Happily never after

He's handsome, they all say.
But frankly
I don't care much for him
because he's my husband.

Would you enjoy ambrosia
if you had to drink it every day
on the doctor's instructions?

Seven Hundred Aryas, Govardhana, 1100 CE, Bengal

Seven Hundred Aryas is Govardhana's experiment in injecting the 'rustic' flavours of Prakrit poetry into high Sanskrit, a task he compares to making a river flow uphill.

187. Things go sour

Thinking myself lucky, I let her reign over my wealth, my home, my people, my body, and even my life. And what did she do? Left me standing in my tighty-whities.

Tales of Ten Young Men, Dandi, 700 CE?, Dravida

Tales of Ten Young Men snappily narrates the adventures of ten young men, and is filled with travel, romance, impersonation, gambling, sorcery, and murder.

188. The story of my cheeks

Back then
when your glance
chanced upon my cheeks
it would stay there
gazing for an eternity.

And now
it's the same old me
and the same old cheeks
but what happened to that glance?

Seven Hundred Gahas, 100 CE?, Deccan

189. Match made in hell

'A grizzly is a bare
a rabbit is a hair
yes, my lady fare
we make a lovely pear.

Today I feel such dead
I mean I feel such red
what I mean is dread.'

To this marvellous head
poor Vikatanitamba was wed.

Commentary on Kavyalankara, 1000 CE

Apart from this unfortunate marriage that we hear about, Vikatanitamba was also unfortunately named ('Ms Ugly Behind'). She is spoken admiringly about by authors of old, but only a few stray verses of hers survive.

190. You can't trust love

Cheer up, girl!
It'll be all right.
Love is fickle
it leaps from one to another
like a monkey in the hills
from tree to tree.

Princess Kuvalayamala, Uddyotana Suri, 700 CE, Gurjara

As an aside, *Princess Kuvalayamala* features a market scene where small snippets of eighteen different languages spoken across the country can be heard. This is our small and only window into the languages actually spoken on the streets in early India. Some of these snippets sound rather like something you might hear today ('tere mere aau').

191. Impossible to please

Anything that
isn't to your liking
I won't do.

But tell me, darling
what can I do
when the thing that
isn't to your liking
is me?

Seven Hundred Gahas, 100 CE?, Deccan

192. Arms race

My love and
your indifference
are in a race
to stay ahead of the other.
Which will end up winning?
It remains to be seen.

Wishing Tree of Rasa, 1700 CE

193. Story of a marriage

I kissed him hard.
My hands were tingling
as I stroked every inch of him.
I wrapped my arms around him
my bangles jangling.

But he only sleeps
and sleeps
and sleeps.
What can I say?
And to whom?

Arrangement of Verses, 1600 CE, Maharashtra

194. Driving a wedge

If you take their names
and burn the feathers
of crows and owls

their love
no matter how strong
will unravel in a trice.

Hara's Girdle, 900 CE, Chittor

The subtext is that the couple will begin to hate each other with a passion, just like crows and owls do.

HOW TO LET GO

195. The human condition

In the great ocean
one log meets another
and having met
they drift apart.

Such is our lot.

Mahabharata, Vyasa

The is amongst the best-known verses of Sanskrit literature, appearing in both the Ramayana and the Mahabharata.

196. Who understands men?

'Isn't this black?'
'Yes, seems like it.'

'Actually, it's white.'
'Oh yes, I see it now.'

'We should get going.'
'I'll get the keys.'

'Or we could stay awhile longer.'
'I'll grab another drink.'

The man who so tangoed
in perfect sync with me
has now turned a perfect stranger.

Does anyone really know men?

Line-up of Good Verse, 1400 CE, Kashmir

There are a great many verses in Sanskrit about the impenetrability of the female mind, but this is perhaps the only one about men. We have modernized the context.

197. After a lifetime of love

After a lifetime of love ripened
over shared joys and shared sorrows
the first to die lives.
It is the other
who's really dead.

Seven Hundred Gahas, 100 CE?, Deccan

198. Nostalgia

Ah, the strange ways of time.

The young man I loved
once spoilt by poetry
now recites scripture.

I too
leave for my husband's.

Seven Hundred Gahas, 100 CE?, Deccan

199. Constant vigilance

'Sir, how must we conduct ourselves with women?'

'Don't see them, Ananda.'

'And if we see them, sir? How must we conduct ourselves then?'

'Don't talk to them, Ananda.'

'And if we talk to them, sir? How must we conduct ourselves then?'

'Practise mindfulness, Ananda.'

Discourse on the Buddha's Passing, 100 BCE?

Ananda was the Buddha's favourite disciple and closest companion.

200. Rose-tinted glasses come off

I knew not
where I ended
and where you began.
Such was love at first.

Then you were my lover
and wistful as I was
I was loved.

Now you are the husband
and I, the spouse.

What can I say?
It's my fault
for going on living.

Treasury of Verse-Jewels, 1000 CE, Bengal

As P.G. Wodehouse famously said, 'Marriage is not a process for prolonging the life of love, sir. It merely mummifies its corpse.'

201. Praying for invisibility

If a woman laughs at a man
with a wink to her friend
and a high-five
may the ground kindly grant him
a hole to be swallowed up by.

Bawd's Counsel, Damodaragupta, 800 CE, Kashmir

Bawd's Counsel is special in having a plot centred around ordinary people, as opposed to most old Indian literature which is dominated by gods, kings and heroes.

202. A lesson in goodbyes

I could say
        'Don't go'
but that's bad luck.
        'See you'?
Love doesn't work that way.
        'Absolutely not'?
That's being bossy.
        'Do as you like'?
That's indifference.
        'I might just die'?
You wouldn't believe it.

Before you leave, darling
teach me how to say goodbye.

Line-up of Good Verse, 1400 CE, Kashmir

It is still considered bad luck in India to stop someone about to leave.

203. Not like it used to be

I was you
and you were me.

What transpired
that now we see

you as you
and me as me?

Bhartrihari's Three Hundred, Bhartrihari, 300 CE?

Legend has it that Bhartrihari was the king of Ujjain who gave up the world when he discovered that his dearest queen actually preferred his stable keeper.

204. Daily heartbreak

Today too
the day has passed
with your heartless father gone.
The streets are shrouded
in darkness.
Come, my little son –
let us sleep.

Line-up of Good Verse, 1400 CE, Kashmir

Melancholic verses like this are rare in Sanskrit, and all the more heart-rending for it.

205. Young adventures

This idol of Ganapati
at its lonely shrine under the tree –

my boyfriends would use it
to give me a makeshift pillow
while we did the deed.

Now, too, I go to that Ganapati
but for my daily prayers.

Growing old stinks.

Seven Hundred Gahas, 100 CE?, Deccan

Such tree-shrines with dilapidated idols are still a common sight in India.

206. Enough of this love nonsense!

My friend Pundarika, I ask you only this. This obsession of yours – is this what your teachers have taught you? Is this what the holy books instruct? Will this help you cultivate dharma? Or penance? Or take you to heaven? Or lead you to moksha? Or is this the secret to fulfilling some vow you have taken up? It is not right to even think it, let alone say it aloud. Love is making a laughingstock of you and you don't even see it. It's only a fool who is taken for a ride by love. What hope do you have of finding pleasure in these things, which good people warn against and ordinary people applaud? A fool who goes after sensual pleasures – which always end in disaster – thinking they will bring him joy is like someone who waters a poisonous plant as a good deed, like someone who runs towards a sword mistaking it for a garland of flowers, like someone who embraces a cobra mistaking it for fragrant smoke, like someone who clasps burning coal thinking it a shining jewel, like someone who picks at the tusks of an elephant submerged in water mistaking them for lotus stalks. Who is this God of love, after all? Be firm and give the scoundrel a good tongue-lashing.

Princess Kadambari, Bana, 600 CE, Kanyakubja

The torrent of Bana's expression sweeps the reader away to a new world where even blades of grass are rendered in ultra-high definition. Bana is to Sanskrit prose what Kalidasa is to verse.

207. No more fairy tales

There's really no such thing
as true love.

If there were
would lovers leave?
And with them gone
would lovers live?

Seven Hundred Gahas, 100 CE?, Deccan

208. Recipe for happiness

No fetter
ensnares like love.
No flood
overpowers like desire.
No fire
burns like passion.

And when you give up these three:
you find happiness.

Sundari and Nanda, Ashvaghosha, 100 CE?

209. 'Tis better to not love at all

Far better
that neither loves
than loving
and not being loved back.

A face is prettier
with no earrings at all
than with just the one.

Pearl Necklace of Verses, 1200 CE, Deccan

210. Neither here nor there

There's one perfect lover –
Shiva
who draws half his darling's body
into his very own.
There's one perfect monk –
the Buddha
who gave up everything
to do with women.

And here we are –
the rest of us
mocked by love
dazed by its poison
not able to spit
not able to swallow.

Bhartrihari's Three Hundred, Bhartrihari, 300 CE?

211. The misery never ends

This anguish wrenches my heart
but stops short of tearing it apart.
My body swoons and faints
but stops short of breathing its last.
The grief blazes strong inside
but stops short of burning me to ash.
Wretched fate's exquisite torture
stops short of taking my life.

Malati and Madhava, Bhavabhuti, 700 CE, Kanyakubja

212. Just one plea

God! Please don't create me again.
If you must, then not as a human being.
If you must, then no love, please.
But if you must, then no long distance.

Madhavanala and Kamakandala, 1400 CE?

213. The three things we hate

The tree of misery
rooted in the bad karma
of a thousand past births
grows three branches:

Waiting on those who are vile.

Seeing those we detest flourish.

And loving those
who won't love us back.

Mallikamakaranda, Ramachandra Suri, 1100 CE, Gurjara

214. Carpe diem

Life is like a drop of water
who knows how long it'll last?
Riches are like waves
who knows when they'll crash?
Love is like a dream
who knows when it'll vanish?

Know this
and do what you will.

Collection of Prakrit Verse

215. Loving too much

First uprooted
dunked in hot water
then crushed

such is the fate of the madder plant
that grows too red.

What can it do
but bear with it?

Apabhramsha Grammar, 1100 CE, Gurjara

A popular red dye was extracted from the root of the madder plant, called manjistha in Sanskrit.

216. Epilogue 1

You may
meditate on the Love God
serve him
bow to him
or even curse him out.

Will he appear with a bang
hand raised in protection
to iron out your love troubles?
Maybe, maybe not.

But if you learn
how these old masters
worked their words,
love will wait upon you
like a faithful servant
doing your every bidding.

Pink slip the useless God
and feed him to the wolves.

217. Epilogue 2

Throw into an old well
those shastras and puranas
which promise you
divine dudes and damsels
in heaven.

If you heed this book
before long
they will come to your arms
right here on earth.

218. Parting benediction

May all the losers swipe left on you.
May your girlfriend pull you tighter in embrace.
May your parents not cast spying glances.

And finally –

may the Love God always
fire his arrows in pairs.

This is our parting benediction.

Thus concludes the anthology
titled *How to Love in Sanskrit*
put together by Anusha and Suhas

Guide to the Transliteration

अ	आ	इ	ई	उ	ऊ	ऋ	ॠ
a	ā	i	ī	u	ū	ṛ	ṝ
ऐ	ए	ऑ	ओ	औ			
ĕ	e	ŏ	o	au			
अँ	अं	अः					
ã	aṃ	aḥ					

क	ख	ग	घ	ङ			
ka	kha	ga	gha	ṅa			
च	छ	ज	झ	ञ			
ca	cha	ja	jha	ñ			
ट	ठ	ड	ढ	ण			
ṭa	ṭha	ḍa	ḍha	ṇa			
त	थ	द	ध	न			
ta	ṭha	da	dha	na			
प	फ	ब	भ	म			
pa	pha	ba	bha	ma			
य	र	ल	व	श	ष	स	ह
ya	ra	la	va	śa	ṣa	sa	ha

This is the same system of sounds that most Indian languages use, apart from a few additional things to consider:

1. The short vowels ĕ and ŏ (ऎ and ऒ). These are the short versions of e and o (ए and ओ).
2. Nasalized vowels are marked with a squiggly line (tilde): ã, ĩ, ũ (अँ, इँ, उँ).
3. Two little dots (umlaut) are used to distinguish the two vowels aï (अइ) from the diphthong ai (ऐ). The same goes for aü (अउ) and au (औ).

List of Verses in the Source Language

- pariṇaya-mālā-vinimaya-samaya-sakalahaṃ catuṣṭayaṃ doṣṇām ǀ duritam apaharatu śaurer ghaṭita-kṣīrodajā-vijayaṃ ǁ *maṅgalācaraṇaṃ suhāsasya* ǀ mālā-vinimaye ahamprathamikayā vadhū-varau spardhete karṇāṭeṣu ǀ

1. eĩ ahara-hariyāruṇima-maraṭṭāĩ lajjamāṇāiṃ ǀ biṃba-phalāiṃ ubbaṃdhaṇaṃ va vallīsu virayaṃti ǁ [etasyāḥ adhara-hṛtāruṇima-garvāṇi lajjamānāni ǀ bimba-phalāni udbandhanam iva vallīṣu viracayanti ǁ] *Kumārapālapratibodha* p. 269
2. uddhaccho piaï jalaṃ jaha jaha viralaṃgulī ciraṃ pahio ǀ pāvāliā vi taha taha dhāraṃ taṇuaṃ pi taṇuei ǁ [ūrdhvākṣaḥ pibati jalaṃ yathā yathā viralāṅguliḥ ciraṃ pathikaḥ ǀ prapā-pālikā api tathā tathā dhārāṃ tanukām api tanūkaroti ǁ] *Gāhāsattasaī* 161
3. yātā locana-gocaraṃ yadi vidher eṇekṣaṇā sundarī neyaṃ kuṅkuma-paṅka-piñjara-mukhī tenojjhitā syāt kṣaṇam ǀ nāpy āmīlita-locanasya racanād rūpaṃ bhaved īdṛśaṃ tasmāt

sarvam akartṛkaṃ jagad idaṃ śreyo mataṃ saugatam ॥
Subhāṣitaratnakośa 440

4. tvāṃ sraṣṭuṃ satṛṇaṃ sadābhyavaharan nārho vidhiḥ prārthito navyo 'nyo nitarām idamprathamatā-'vaidagdhya-śikṣākulaḥ। sollekhā ca ghuṇākṣarīṇa-sadṛśī vaktuṃ na yuktā sthitiḥ tvat-sargānumitau vimuhyati tarām itthaṃ janaḥ tārkikaḥ ॥ *Sūktāvali* (Folio 10 recto, line 3). Some emendations have been made.
5. vilokitāsyā mukham unnamayya kiṃ vedhaseyaṃ suṣamā-samāptau? । dhṛtyudbhavā yac cibuke cakāsti nimne manāg aṅguli-yantraṇeva ॥ *Naiṣadhīyacarita* 7.51
6. stana-yugam atīva-tuṅgaṃ nimno madhyaḥ samunnataṃ jaghanam । iti viṣame hariṇākṣyā vapuṣi nave ka iva na skhalati? ॥ *Śārṅgadharapaddhati* 3370
7. jassa jahiṃ cia paḍhamaṃ tissā aṃgammi ṇivaḍiā diṭṭhī । tassa tahiṃ cea ṭhiā savvaṃgaṃ keṇa vi ṇa diṭṭhaṃ ॥ [yasya yatraiva prathamaṃ tasyāḥ ange nipatitā dṛṣṭiḥ । tasya tatraiva sthitā sarvāṅgaṃ kenāpi na dṛṣṭaṃ ॥] *Gāhāsattasaī* 234
8. dṛṣṭiṃ dehi punar bāle! kamalāyata-locane! । śrūyate hi purā loke viṣasya viṣam auṣadham ॥ *Śṛṅgāratilaka* 15
9. eīe bālāe loyaṇa-lāyanna-lāha-luddhāiṃ । muddhāī maya-kulāiṃ vaṇa-vāsa-vayaṃ va sevaṃti ॥ [etasyāḥ bālāyāḥ locana-lāvaṇya-lābha-lubdhāni । mugdhāni mṛga-kulāni vana-vāsa-vratam iva sevante ॥] *Kumārapālapratibodha* p. 269
10. locane hariṇa-garva-mocane mā vibhūṣaya natāṅgi! kajjalaiḥ । eka eva yadi jīva-hārakaḥ sāyako na garalena lipyate ॥ *Rasikajīvana* 4.34
11. virājate 'syās tilako 'yam añcito vikuñcita-bhrū-latikāntare nṛpa! । vijitya loka-dvitayaṃ divaṃ prati smareṇa bāṇo dhanuṣīva saṃhitaḥ ॥ *Navasāhasāṅkacarita* 7.15
12. etat te bhrū-latollāsi pāṭalādhara-pallavam । mukhaṃ nandanam udyānam ato 'nyat kevalaṃ vanaṃ ॥ *Nāgānanda* 3.11

13. tapasyatīva candro 'yaṃ tvan-mukhendu-jigīṣayā । kṛśaḥ śambhu-jaṭā-jūṭa-taṭinī-taṭam āśritaḥ ॥ *Subhāṣitaratnakośa* 460

14. ghariṇīa mahāṇasa-kamma-lagga-masi-maïlieṇa hattheṇa । chittaṃ muhaṃ hasijjaï caṃdāvatthaṃ gaaṃ païṇā ॥ [gṛhiṇyāḥ mahānasa-karma-lagna-masi-malinitena hastena । spṛṣṭaṃ mukhaṃ hasyate candrāvasthāṃ gataṃ patyā ॥] *Gāhāsattasaī* 14

15. tuha muhasāricchaṃ ṇa lahaï tti saṃpuṇṇa-maṃḍalo vihiṇā । aṇṇamaaṃ va ghaḍeuṃ puṇo vi khaṃḍijjaï miaṃko ॥ [tava mukha-sādṛśyaṃ na labhate iti sampūrṇa-maṇḍalo vidhinā । punaruktam iva ghaṭayituṃ punar api khaṇḍyate mṛgāṅkaḥ ॥] *Gāhāsattasaī* 207

16. kālakkhara! dusikkhia! dhammia! re ṇiṃba-kīḍaa-saricchā! । dōṇṇa vi ṇiraa-ṇivāso samaaṃ jaï hoi tahi hodu ॥ [kālākṣara! duḥśikṣita! dhārmika! re nimba-kīṭa-sadṛkṣa! । dvayor api niraya-nivāsaḥ samaṃ yadi bhavati tad bhavatu ॥] *Gāhāsattasaī* 878

17. paśyāyatākṣi! bhuvana-tritayaika-jiṣṇoḥ śikṣā-balaṃ dhanuṣi śambara-śāsanasya । bhittvā mamaiva hṛdayaṃ hṛdaye niviṣṭā bāṇā yad atrabhavatīṃ na khalu spṛśanti ॥ *Subhāṣitasudhānidhi* 32.7

18. natāṅgyā man-manaḥ-kāṭhinyam ākhyātam । yadā keli-vane kuraṅga-locanā locana-patham avartata tadaiva apahṛta-madīya-mānasā sā sva-mandiram agāt । sā cetaso mādhurya-kāṭhinye svayam eva jānāti । *Daśakumāracarita* 5.59

19. iha sphuṭaṃ tiṣṭhati nātha! kaṇṭakaṃ śanaiś śanaiḥ karṣa nakhāgra-līlayā । iti cchalāt kācid alagna-kaṇṭakaṃ padaṃ tad-utsaṅga-tale nyaveśayat ॥ *Śārṅgadharapaddhati* 3582

20. kāmo vāma-svabhāvena pratikūleṣu vardhate abhilāṣaṃ hinasty eṣa svādhīneṣu saraḥ smaraḥ । ata eva vidagdhena durlabhatvaṃ prayatnataḥ kartavyaṃ dhīra-vṛttena sukha-sāmrājyam icchatā ॥ *Mānasollāsa*, Vol. 3, 1021–22

21. smartavyo ’haṃ tvayā kānte na smariṣyāmy ahaṃ tava । yena tvāṃ saṃsmariṣyāmi hṛdayaṃ tat tvayā hṛtam ॥ *Subhāṣitāvalī* 1044

22. śikhariṇi kva nu nāma kiyac ciraṃ kimabhidhānam asāv akarot tapaḥ? । taruṇi! yena tavādhara-pāṭalaṃ daśati bimba-phalaṃ śuka-śāvakaḥ ॥ *Dhvanyāloka* p. 58

23. “kanye! kāmayamānaṃ māṃ na tvaṃ kāmayase katham?” । iti grāmyo ’yam arthātmā vairasyāyaiva kalpate ॥ “kāmaṃ kandarpa-caṇḍālo mayi vāmākṣi! niṣṭhuraḥ । tvayi nirmatsaro diṣṭye” ty agrāmyo ’rtho rasāvahaḥ ॥ *Kāvyādarśa* 1.63–64

24. ámo ’hám asmi sā́ tvaṃ sā́māhám asmy ṛ́k tváṃ dyáur aháṃ pṛthivī́ tvam । tā́v ihá sáṃ bhavāva prajā́m ā́ janayāvahai ॥ *Atharvaveda* 14.2.71

25. sūracchaleṇa puttaa! kassa tumaṃ aṃjaliṃ paṇāmesi? । hāsa-kaḍakkhummissā ṇa hŏṃti devāṇa jŏkkārā ॥ [sūrya-cchalena putraka! kasya tvam añjalim arpayasi? । hāsa-kaṭākṣonmiśrāḥ na bhavanti devānāṃ jyotkārāḥ ॥] *Gāhāsattasaī* 332

26. akṣa-devana-paṇīkṛte ‘dhare kāntayor jaya-parājaye sati । atra vaktu yadi vetti manmathaḥ kas tayor jayati jīyate ‘thavā ॥ *Subhāṣitāvalī* 2048

27. āśleṣe prathamaṃ kramād apahṛte hṛdye ‘dharasyārpaṇe keli-dyūta-vidhau paṇaṃ priyatame kāntāṃ punaḥ pṛcchati । antar-gūḍha-vigāḍha-sambhrama-rasa-sphārībhavad-gaṇḍayā tūṣṇīṃ śāri-visāraṇāya nihitaḥ svedāmbu-garbhaḥ karaḥ ॥ *Subhāṣitaratnakośa* 605

28. “akṣa-dyūta-jitādhara-graha-vidhāv īśo ’si tat-khaṇḍanād ādhikye vada ko bhavān?” iti mṛṣā kopāñcita-bhrū-latam । svidyat-khinna-karāgra-kuḍmala-parāyattīkṛtāsyasya me mugdhākṣī pratikṛtya tat kṛtavatī dyūte ’pi yan nārjitam ॥ *Sūktimuktāvalī* 75.6

29. śayyāgāraṃ vrajantyāś catura-sahacarī-mugdhamugdhokti-miśraṃ prāṇeśāyāḥ smara-jyā-raṇitam iva samākarṇya mañjīra-ghoṣam ॥ yāminyāḥ pūrva-yāme vigalati vitatautsukyam

ujjṛmbhamāṇo dhanyo nidrā-cchalena ślathayati suhṛdām narma-goṣṭhī-prabandham ॥ *Saduktikarṇāmṛta* 1041

30. addhacchi-pĕcchiaṃ mā karehi sāhāviaṃ paloehi । so vi sudiṭṭho hohii tumaṃ pi muddhā kalijjihisi ॥ [ardhākṣi-prekṣitaṃ mā kuru svābhāvikaṃ pralokaya । so 'pi sudṛṣṭo bhaviṣyati tvam api mugdhā kaliṣyase ॥] *Gāhāsattasaī* 225

31. pṛṣṭhe kañcuka-muktyai sutanur asavyaṃ prahiṇvatī pāṇim । hantum iva citta-hariṇaṃ yūnaḥ tūṇād iveṣum ādatte ॥ *Rasikajīvana* 7.88

32. aṇṇaṃ taṃ ṇūmijjaï eam puṇa suaṇu vammaha-rahassam । paaḍijjantaṃ ṇa tahā guppantaṃ jaha phuḍīhoi ॥ [anyat tad gupyate etat punaḥ sutanu! manmatha-rahasyam । prakaṭyamānaṃ na tathā gupyamānaṃ yathā sphuṭībhavati ॥] *Līlāvaī* 499

33. sahasa tti jaṃ na diṭṭho sarahasa-cittena jaṃ na ālatto । uvayāro jaṃ ṇa kao taṃ ciya kaliyaṃ chaïllehiṃ ॥ [sahasā yan na dṛṣṭaḥ sarabhasa-cittena yan na ālapitaḥ । upacāro yan na kṛtaḥ tad eva kalitaṃ vidagdhaiḥ ॥] *Gāhārayaṇakoso* 257

34. nihnavanīyaṃ kiñcit kiñcin mugdhe! prakāśanīyaṃ ca । saṃvibhajati patyārdhād adhikaṃ na nagādhirājatanayāpi ॥ Unpublished. By Suhas Mahesh.

35. asatī kulajā dhīrā prauḍhā prativeśinī yadāsaktim । kurute sarasā ca tadā brahmānandaṃ tṛṇaṃ manye ॥ *Āryāsaptaśatī* 70

36. maṇṇe āaṇṇaṃtā āsaṇṇa-vivāha-maṃgaluggīaṃ । tehi juāṇehi samaṃ hasaṃti maṃ veasa-kuḍuṃgā ॥ [manye ākarṇayantaḥ āsanna-vivāha-maṅgalodgītam । taiḥ yuvabhiḥ samaṃ hasanti mām vetasa-nikuñjāḥ ॥] *Gāhāsattasaī* 645

37. priye! karṇejapa-trāsāt prema tyaktuṃ kim icchasi? । ko 'pi likṣā-bhaya-trāsāj jahāti vasanaṃ janaḥ? ॥ *Vidyākarasahasraka* 616

38. muha-vijjhavia-paīvaṃ ṇiruddha-sāsaṃ sa-saṃkiullāvaṃ । savaha-saa-rakkhiŏṭṭhaṃ coria-ramiaṃ suhāvei ॥ [mukha-

vidhmāpita-pradīpaṃ niruddha-śvāsaṃ saśaṅkitollāpam ।
śapatha-śata-rakṣitoṣṭhaṃ caurya-rataṃ sukhayati ॥]
Gāhāsattasaī 333

39. smara-rasa-nadī-pūreṇoḍhāḥ punar guru-setubhir yadapi vidhṛtās tiṣṭhanty ārād apūrṇa-manorathāḥ । tadapi likhita-prakhyair aṅgaiḥ parasparam unmukhā nayana-nalinī-nālānītaṃ pibanti rasaṃ priyāḥ ॥ *Amaruśataka* 104

40. kaccit priya smarasi māṃ vaṭa-vṛkṣa-mūle gantuṃ purīṃ vyavasite tvayi śikṣaṇārtham । tvāṃ draṣṭum āgatavatīṃ janakāt prabhītāṃ vṛṣṭyātapāvṛta-dharām iva sasmitāsrām ॥ *patipatnīsallāpa* 14

41. "āvayoḥ saṅgamo nātha! punaḥ kutra bhaviṣyati?" । "dharma-śāstraṃ pramāṇaṃ cet kumbhīpāke bhaviṣyati" ॥ Orally transmitted

42. āstāṃ viśvasanaṃ sakhīṣu viditābhiprāya-sāre jane tatrāpy arpayituṃ dṛśaṃ suracitāṃ śaknomi na vrīḍayā । loko 'py eṣa paropahāsa-caturaḥ sūkṣmeṅgita-jño 'py alaṃ mātaḥ! kaṃ śaraṇaṃ vrajāmi hṛdaye jīrṇo 'nurāgānalaḥ ॥ *Amaruśataka* 63

43. dampatyor niśi jalpator gṛha-śukenākarṇitaṃ yad vacaḥ tat prātar guru-sannidhau nigadataḥ śrutvaiva tāraṃ vadhūḥ । karṇālambita-padmarāga-śakalaṃ vinyasya cañcvāḥ puro vrīḍārtā prakaroti dāḍima-phala-vyājena vāg-bandhanam ॥ *Amaruśataka* 16

44. "kva prasthitāsi karabhoru! ghane niśīthe?" "prāṇādhiko vasati yatra janaḥ priyo me" । "ekākinī bata! kathaṃ na bibheṣi? bāle!" "nanv asti puṅkhita-śaro madanaḥ sahāyaḥ" ॥ *Amaruśataka* 71

45. alasa-valitaiḥ premārdrārdrair muhur mukulīkṛtaiḥ kṣaṇam abhimukhair lajjā-lolair nimeṣa-parāṅmukhaiḥ । hṛdaya-nihitaṃ bhāvākūtaṃ vamadbhir ivekṣaṇaiḥ kathaya sukṛtī ko 'yaṃ mugdhe tvayādya vilokyate? ॥ *Amaruśataka* 4

46. vaṃka-bhaṇiyāĩ katto katto addhacchi-picchiyavvāiṃ? ı ūsasiyaṃ pi muṇijjai chaïlla-jaṇa-saṃkule gāme ıı [vakra-bhaṇitāni kutaḥ kutaḥ ardhākṣi-prekṣitavyāni? ı ucchvasitam api jñāyate vidagdha-jana-saṅkule grāme ıı] *Gāhārayaṇakoso* 255

47. sūī-vehe musalaṃ vicchuhamāṇeṇa ḍaḍḍha-loeṇa ı ĕkka-ggāme vi pio samehi acchīhi vi ṇa diṭṭho ıı [sūci-vedhe musalaṃ vikṣipatā dagdha-lokena ı eka-grāme 'pi priyaḥ samābhyām akṣibhyām api na dṛṣṭaḥ ıı] *Gāhāsattasaī* 502

48. pariosa-viasiehiṃ bhaṇiaṃ acchīhi teṇa jaṇa-majjhe ı paḍivaṇṇaṃ tīa vi uvvamaṃta-seehi aṃgehiṃ ıı [paritoṣa-vikasitaiḥ bhaṇitam akṣibhyāṃ tena jana-madhye ı pratipannaṃ tayāpi udvamat-svedaiḥ aṅgaiḥ ıı] *Gāhāsattasaī* 341

49. puṣpaṃ pravālopahitaṃ yadi syān muktāphalaṃ vā sphuṭa-vidruma-stham ı tato 'nukuryād viśadasya tasyāḥ tāmrauṣṭha-paryasta-rucaḥ smitasya ıı *Kumārasambhava* 1.43

50. yad eva rocate mahyaṃ tad eva kurute priyā ı iti vetti na jānāti tat priyaṃ yat karoti sā ıı *Śṛṅgāraprakāśa* 22.7, p. 1099

51. ĕddaha-mĕttammi jae suṃdara-mahilā-sahassa-bharie vi ı aṇuharaï ṇavara tissā vāmaddhaṃ dāhiṇaddhassa ıı [etāvan-mātre jagati sundara-mahilā-sahasra-bhṛte 'pi ı anuharati kevalaṃ tasyāḥ vāmārdhaṃ dakṣiṇārdhasya ıı] *Gāhāsattasaī* 303

52. vātsyāyana-madanodaya-dattaka-viṭavṛtta-rājaputrādyaiḥ ı ucchvasitaṃ yatkiñcit tat tasyā hṛdaya-deśam adhyāste ıı *Kuṭṭanīmata* 123

53. līneva pratibimbiteva likhitevotkīrṇa-rūpeva ca pratyupteva ca vajralepa-ghaṭitevāntar-nikhāteva ca ı sā naḥ cetasi kīliteva viśikhaiḥ cetobhuvaḥ pañcabhiḥ cintā-santati-tantu-jāla-nibiḍa-syūteva lagnā priyā ıı *Mālatīmādhava* 5.10

54. viniścetuṃ śakyo na sukham iti vā duḥkham iti vā pramoho nidrā vā kimu viṣa-visarpaḥ kimu madaḥ। tava sparśe sparśe mama hi parimūḍhendriya-gaṇo vikāraḥ ko 'py antar jaḍayati ca tāpaṃ ca kurute ॥ *Uttararāmacarita* 1.35. The final line is taken from a quotation in Daśarūpaka 4.69.

55. ahara-cchaleṇa dinnā vihiṇā siṃdūra-rāyamudda vva। vayaṇe biṃba-nihā se lāyannaṃ rakkhamāṇeṇa ॥ [adhara-cchalena dattā vidhinā sindūra-rājamudrā iva। vadane bimba-nibhā asyāḥ lāvaṇyaṃ rakṣatā ॥] *Gāhārayaṇakoso* 305

56. hāro 'yaṃ hariṇākṣīṇāṃ luṭhati stana-maṇḍale। muktānām apy avastheyaṃ ke vayaṃ smara-kiṅkarāḥ? ॥ *Subhāṣitaratnakośa* 479

57. daśana-vasane lauhityena staneṣu tathoṣmaṇā madhupa-paṭalī-dhūmre dhūmaśriyā kabarī-bhare। saruṣi hṛdaye tāsāṃ jvālākulair dṛśi kajjalair iti pariṇaman kandarpāgnir vibhakta ivābhavat ॥ *Kapphiṇābhyudaya* 14.23

58. tvaṃ dūram api gacchantī hṛdayaṃ na jahāsi me। dināvasāne chāyeva puro mūlaṃ vanaspateḥ ॥ *Rasakalpadruma,* p.143

59. kim aśakanīyaṃ premṇaḥ? phaṇinaḥ kathayāpi yā bibheti sma। sā giriśa-bhuja-bhujaṅgama-phaṇopadhānādya nidrāti ॥ *Āryāsaptaśatī* 159

60. maha païṇā thaṇa-juale pattaṃ lihiaṃ ti gavviā kīsa?। ālihaï mahaṃ pi pio jaï se kaṃpŏ ccia ṇa hoi ॥ [mama patyā stana-yugale pattraṃ likhitam iti garvitā kasmāt?। ālikhati mamāpi priyaḥ yadi tasya kampaḥ eva na bhavati ॥] *Gāhāsattasaī* 830

61. api dayita! smarasi purā tvayeritaṃ mayi nilīya nayana-yuge। "preyasi! mayālikhitacirakavitānāṃ tvam asi sampuṭī" ti mudā ॥ *Ujjvalajvālā* 37

62. pathi pathika-vadhūbhiḥ sādaraṃ pṛcchyamānā "kuvalaya-dala-nīlaḥ ko 'yam ārye! tave" ti। smita-vikasita-gaṇḍaṃ vrīḍa-vibhrānta-netraṃ mukham avanamayantī spaṣṭam ācaṣṭa sītā ॥ *Hanumannāṭaka* 3.15

63. pimmaṃ taṃ ciya jāyaṃti jattha dosā vi naṇu guṇa cceya ı siddha-raso so kira jattha huṃti lohāĩ vi suvannaṃ ıı [prema tad eva jāyante yatra doṣāḥ api nanu guṇāḥ eva ı siddharasaḥ sa kila yatra bhavanti lohāny api suvarṇam ıı] *Subhāsiapajjasaṃgaha* 70

64. nūnam ājñā-karas tasyāḥ subhruvo makaradhvajaḥ ı yatas tan-netra-sañcāra-sūciteṣu pravartate ıı *Subhāṣitaratnakośa* 489

65. dhanyāsi yat kathayasi priya-saṅgame 'pi narma-smitaṃ ca vadanaṃ ca rasaṃ ca tasya ı nīvīṃ prati praṇihite tu kare priyeṇa sakhyaḥ! śapāmi yadi kiñcid api smarāmi ıı *Saduktikarṇāmṛta* 1172

66. ṇŏkkhī bhallī sa vaṃmahe ṇimmia taĩlŏkke vi ı jehĩ vimukkī te vi mua jāhã ṇa laggī te vi ıı [abhinavā bhallī sā manmathena nirmitā trailokye 'pi ı yeṣu vimuktā te 'pi mṛtāḥ yeṣāṃ na lagnā te 'pi ıı] *Śṛṅgāraprakāśa* 9.8, Vol .1, p. 453. This is an Apabhramsha doha. We have further restored the text using V.M. Kulkarni's restoration as a guideline.

67. na jāne saṃmukhāyāte priyāṇi vadati priye ı sarvāṇy aṅgāni kiṃ yānti netratāṃ kimu karṇatām ıı *Amaruśataka* 64

68. svabhyasta-rūpāpi naveva nityaṃ vināpi hāsaṃ hasatīva kāntyā ı madād ṛte 'pi skhalatīva bhāvair vācaṃ vinā vyāharatīva dṛṣṭyā ıı *Mahābhārata* 1.179.22b*1851

69. caṃda-sarisaṃ muhaṃ se saraso amaassa muha-raso tissā ı sakaa-ggaha-rahasujjala-cuṃvaṇaaṃ kassa sarisaṃ se? ıı [candra-sadṛśaṃ mukhaṃ tasyāḥ sadṛśo amṛtasya mukha-raso tasyāḥ ı sakaca-graha-rabhasojjvala-cumbanaṃ kasya sadṛśaṃ tasyāḥ? ıı] *Gāhāsattasaī* 213

70. talpe prabhur iva gurur iva manasija-tantre śrame bhujiṣyeva ı gehe śrīr iva guru-jana-purato mūrteva sā vrīḍā ıı *Āryāsaptaśatī* 257

71. preyo mitraṃ bandhutā vā samagrā sarve kāmāḥ sampado jīvitaṃ vā । strīṇāṃ bhartā dharma-dārāś ca puṃsām ity anyonyaṃ vatsayor jñātam astu ॥ *Mālatīmādhava* 6.18

72. tāṭaṅkam asyās taralekṣaṇāyā muktāphalaiḥ cāru rucaṃ vidhatte । mukha-śriyā candram ivābhibhūya bandīkṛtaṃ tāraka-cakravālam ॥ *Śārṅgadharapaddhati* 3308

73. śyāmāsv aṅgaṃ cakita-hariṇī-prekṣaṇe dṛṣṭi-pātaṃ vaktra-cchāyāṃ śaśini śikhināṃ barha-bhāreṣu keśān । utpaśyāmi pratanuṣu nadī-vīciṣu bhrū-vilāsān hantaikasmin kvacid api na te caṇḍi! sādṛśyam asti ॥ *Meghadūta* 2.44

74. priyāyā virahe rāmo babandha saritāmpatim । ahaṃ nayanajaṃ vāri niroddhum api na kṣamaḥ ॥ *Vidyākarasahasraka* 397

75. pañcatvaṃ tanur etu bhūta-nivahāḥ svāṃśān viśantu prabho! dhātas! tvāṃ śirasā praṇamya kuru mām ity adya yāce punaḥ । tad-vāpīṣu payaḥ tadīya-makure jyotiḥ tadīyālaya-vyomni vyoma tadīya-vartmani dharāṃ tat-tāla-vṛnte 'nilaṃ ॥ *Subhāṣitāvalī* 1355

76. kuvalaya-nayanā-kucāntareṣu kṣaṇam api yeṣu na śerate yuvānaḥ । śiva! śiva! karuṇā-parāṅmukho 'yaṃ gaṇayati tāny api vāsarāṇi vedhāḥ ॥ *Padyaracanā* 6.16

77. prāsāde sā diśi diśi ca sā pṛṣṭhataḥ sā puraḥ sā paryaṅke sā pathi pathi ca sā tad-viyogāturasya । haṃho cetaḥ prakṛtir aparā nāsti me kāpi sā sā sā sā sā sā jagati sakale ko 'yam advaita-vādaḥ ॥ *Amaruśataka* 102

78. dhanyās te khalu jantavo dayitayā viśleṣam āpadya ye tat-sandarśana-gāḍha-saṃskṛta-dṛśaḥ paśyanti tāḥ sarvataḥ । cetaḥ kintu tayā tathā mama kim apy aikadhyam abhyāgataṃ yenāhaṃ vyatireka-darśanakṛte naitāṃ vivektuṃ kṣamaḥ ॥ Sūktāvali (Folio 10 verso, line 3).

79. tvām ālikhya praṇaya-kupitāṃ dhātu-rāgaiḥ śilāyām ātmānaṃ te caraṇa-patitaṃ yāvad icchāmi kartum । asraiḥ tāvan muhur

upacitair dṛṣṭir ālupyate me krūraḥ tasminn api na sahate saṅgamaṃ nau kṛtāntaḥ ॥ *Meghadūta* 2.45

80. svasti । amuka-sthāne vinirjita-makara-dhvaja-lāvaṇyān autsukyaudārya-saubhāgyādi-guṇa-gaṇāpahṛta-yuvati-mānasān vallabha-amukapādān amuka-sthānāt sadādeśa-kāriṇī amukā sasnehaṃ sotkaṇṭhaṃ gāḍham āliṅgya sāśraṃ vijñapayati yathā । kāryaṃ ca । kuśalam atra । tatratyātmīya-kuśalatā-kiṃvadantībhir anavaratam aham ānandanīyā । yad-dine yuṣmākaṃ vijayayātrā jātā tad-dina-pūrvaṃ viraha-duḥkhānalena tapyamāna-mānasā rātrin-divaṃ saukhyaṃ kvāpi nānutiṣṭhāmi । tathā coktam–viraha-huyāsa-karāliyaha kahi piyayama! kahĩ jaṃpa? । jāva na raï-rasi vimali jali pema-ddahi kiya jhaṃpa ॥ [viraha-hutāśa-karālitāyāḥ kathaya priyatama! kutra śāntiḥ? । yāvan na rati-rase vimala-jale prema-hrade kṛtā jhaṃpā ॥] ityādi paribhāvya mamopari dayāṃ dhṛtvā bahūny api prayojanāni muktvā atrāgatya nija-darśanāmṛta-varṣeṇa vipralambha-pāvaka-dahyamānaṃ madīyam aṅgaṃ nirvāpaṇīyam । kāla-kṣepo na kartavyaḥ ॥ *Lekhapaddhati* p. 63

81. dyūte paṇaḥ praṇaya-keliṣu kaṇṭha-pāśaḥ krīḍā-pariśrama-haraṃ vyajanaṃ ratānte । śayyā niśītha-kalahe hariṇekṣaṇāyāḥ prāptaṃ mayā vidhi-vaśād idam uttarīyam ॥ *Kundamālā* 4.20

82. pāṇḍur asi niśi na śeṣe pratidinam āviṣkaroṣi tanimānam । vayam iva kiṃ tvam api sakhe! śaśāṅka! tām eva cintayasi? ॥ *Subhāṣitāvalī* 1260

83. baïṭṭho ṭhakkuro, kkhuhā-kilanto bahmaṇo, aviṇīda-hiaā bāla-raṇḍā, virahido a māṇuso maṇoraha-modaehiṃ attāṇaṃ viḍambedi । [bhraṣṭo rājā kṣudhā-klānto brāhmaṇo 'vinīta-hṛdayā bāla-raṇḍā virahitaḥ ca mānuṣo manoratha-modakair ātmānaṃ viḍambayati ॥] *Karpūramañjarī* p. 76

84. hāro nāropitaḥ kaṇṭhe mayā viśleṣa-bhīruṇā । idānīm āvayor madhye sarit-sāgara-bhūdharāḥ ॥ *Saduktikarṇāmṛta* 902

85. vāhi vāta! yataḥ kanyā tāṃ spṛṣṭvā mām api spṛśa । tvayi me gātra-saṃsparśaḥ candre dṛṣṭi-samāgamaḥ ॥ *Rāmāyaṇa* 6.5.6

86. vijñaptir eṣā mama jīva-bandho! tatraiva neyā divasāḥ kiyantaḥ । sampraty ayogya-sthitir eṣa deśaḥ karā himāṃśor api tāpayanti ॥ *Saduktikarṇāmṛta* 754

87. bhittvā sadyaḥ kisalaya-puṭān devadāru-drumāṇāṃ ye tat-kṣīra-sruti-surabhayo dakṣiṇena pravṛttāḥ । āliṅgyante guṇavati mayā te tuṣārādri-vātāḥ pūrvaṃ spṛṣṭaṃ yadi kila bhaved aṅgam ebhis taveti ॥ *Meghadūta* 2.47

88. kurvantī svakapola-paṭṭaka-tale cintāmayenātmanā śaśvat-pāṇi-talāvamardana-vaśa-prodbhūta-tāmra-tviṣi । saṅkrāntāṅguli-parva-kīrṇa-rucira-spaṣṭākṣarālīm imāṃ tvaṃ saubhāgya-yaśaḥ-praśastim alikhaḥ kasyeha puṇyātmanaḥ? ॥ Sūktāvali (Folio 10 verso, line 10).

89. yeṣāṃ vallabhayā saha kṣaṇam iva kṣipraṃ kṣapā kṣīyate teṣāṃ śīta-karaḥ śaśī virahiṇām ulkeva santāpakṛt । asmākaṃ tu na vallabhā na virahaḥ tenobhaya-bhraṃśinām indū rājati darpaṇākṛtir asau noṣṇo na vā śītalaḥ ॥ *Prabandhacintāmaṇi* dvitīyaḥ prakāśaḥ 77

90. likhantī sarva-gātrāṇi bhittau patyur viyoginī । caraṇau na likhaty eṣā punar-gamana-śaṅkayā ॥ *Vidyākarasahasraka* 407

91. kāmo hanta! mad-antaraṅga-hariṇaṃ kāñcī-maṇī-kiṅkiṇī-kvāṇa-bhrāntam udāra-rāga-kuhanā-dīpaṃ sakhe! dīpayan । snehodvīkṣaṇa-vāgurāsu patitaṃ tasyā nijair āśugair vyādhaṃ vyādham aho viyoga-dahane śūlākaroti sphuṭam ॥ *Subhadrāpariṇaya* 2.71

92. bahv etat kāmayānasya śakyam etena jīvitum । yad ahaṃ sā ca vāmorur ekāṃ dharaṇim āśritau ॥ *Rāmāyaṇa* 6.5.10

93. jaï kevã i pāvīsu piu akiā kuḍḍu karīsu । pāṇiu navaï sarāvi jivā savvaṃgẽ païsīsu ॥ [yadi katham api prāpsyāmi priyam akṛtaṃ kautukaṃ kariṣyāmi । pānīyaṃ nave śarāve yathā sarvāṅgena pravekṣyāmi ॥] *Siddhahemaśabdānuśāsana* sūtra 396

94. punar api milanaṃ yadākadācit priyatamayā kṛpayā bhaved vidhātuḥ । harir iva karavai hṛdi pratiṣṭhāṃ hara iva kiṃ tanavai tanor abhinnām? ॥ *Padyaracanā* 269

95. priyasakhi! vipad-daṇḍa-prānta-prapāta-paramparā-paricaya-cale cintā-cakre nidhāya vidhiḥ khalaḥ । mṛdam iva balāt piṇḍīkṛtya pragalbha-kulālavad bhramayati mano no jānīmaḥ kim atra vidhāsyati ॥ *Subhāṣitāvalī* 2386

96. jaṃ jaṃ ālihaï maṇo āsāvattīhi hiaa-phalaammi । taṃ taṃ vālŏ vva vihī ṇihuaṃ hasiūṇa pamhusaï ॥ [yat yat ālikhati manaḥ āśā-vartikābhiḥ hṛdayaphalake । tat tat bāla iva vidhiḥ nibhṛtam hasitvā pramṛśati ॥] *Gāhāsattasaī* 658

97. vallaha-jaṇassa dukkhe nisue virahammi jāyae sukkhaṃ । sukkhammi puṇo dukkhaṃ pimmassa gaī aho visamā ॥ [vallabha-janasya duḥkhe niśrute virahe jāyate sukham । sukhe punaḥ duḥkhaṃ premṇaḥ gatiḥ aho viṣamā ॥] *Subhāsiapajjasaṃgaha* 10

98. ajjaṃ cea paüttho ajjaṃ cia suṇṇaāi jāāiṃ । racchāmuha-deula-caccarāi amhaṃ ca hiaāiṃ ॥ [adyaiva proṣitaḥ adyaiva śūnyāni jātāni । rathyāmukha-devakula-catvarāṇi asmākaṃ ca hṛdayāni ॥] *Gāhāsattasaī* 190

99. nadyā iva pravāho viṣama-śilā-saṅkaṭa-skhalita-vegaḥ । vighnita-samāgama-sukho manasiśayaḥ śata-guṇī-bhavati ॥ *Vikramorvaśīya* 3.8

100. "kuśalaṃ tasyā?" "jīvati" "kuśalaṃ pṛṣṭāsi" "jīvatīty uktam" । "punar api tad eva kathayasi" "mṛtāṃ nu kathayāmi yā śvasiti?" ॥ *Saduktikarṇāmṛta* 628

101. adṛṣṭe darśanotkaṇṭhā dṛṣṭe viccheda-bhīrutā । nādṛṣṭena na dṛṣṭena bhavatā labhyate sukham ॥ *Subhāṣitāvalī* 1043

102. viramata viramata sakhyo! nalinī-dala-tāla-vṛnta-pavanena । hṛdaya-gato 'yaṃ vahnir jhaṭiti kadācij jvalaty eva ॥ *Subhāṣitāvalī* 1070

103. śabdākhyeyaṃ yad api kila te yaḥ sakhīnāṃ purastāt karṇe lolaḥ kathayitum abhūd ānana-sparśa-lobhāt ı so 'tikrāntaḥ śravaṇa-viṣayaṃ locanābhyām adṛṣṭaḥ tvām utkaṇṭhā-viracita-padaṃ manmukhenedam āha ॥ *Meghadūta* 2.43

104. vṛthā gāthā-ślokair alam alam alīkāṃ mama rujaṃ kadācid dhūrto 'sau kavi-vacanam ity ākalayati ı idaṃ pārśve tasya prahiṇu sakhi! lagnāñjana-lava-sravad-bāṣpotpīḍa-grathita-lipi tāḍaṅka-yugalam ॥ *Saduktikarṇāmṛta* 607

105. kiṃ bhaṇaha maṃ? sahīo! mā mara dīsihaï so jiaṃtīe ı kajjālāo eso siṇeha-maggo uṇa ṇa hoi ॥ [kiṃ bhaṇatha māṃ? sakhyaḥ! mā mriyasva drakṣyate sa jīvantyā ı kāryālāpaḥ esa sneha-mārgaḥ punar na bhavati ॥] *Gāhāsattasaī* 619

106. adṛṣṭvā tvan-mukhāmbhojam apītvā tvad-vaco'mṛtam ı jīvitaṃ tvābhito 'bhūtvā yat svalpam api tad bahu ॥ atvad-bāhu-śirodhāno 'py atvat-keśa-niśā-gataḥ ı supto 'tvat-kroḍa-saṅkrīḍo yat svalpam api tad bahu ॥ Unpublished. By Balram Shukla.

107. pariosa-suṃdarāiṃ suraesu lahaṃti jāi sŏkkhāi ı tāiṃ cia uṇa virahe khāuggiṇṇāi kīraṃti ॥ [paritoṣa-sundarāṇi surateṣu labhyante yāni saukhyāni ı tāni eva punar virahe khāditodgīrṇāni kriyante ॥] *Gāhāsattasaī* 670

108. saṅgama-viraha-vikalpe varam iha viraho na saṅgamaḥ tasyāḥ ı saṅge saiva tathaikā tribhuvanam api tanmayaṃ virahe ॥ *Saduktikarṇāmṛta* 929

109. netrendīvariṇī mukhāmburuhiṇī bhrū-valli-kallolinī bāhu-dvandva-mṛṇālinī yadi vadhūr vāpī punaḥ sā bhavet ı tal-lāvaṇya-jalāvagāhana-jaḍair aṅgair anaṅgānala-jvālā-jāla-mucaḥ tyajeyam asamāḥ prāṇa-cchido vedanāḥ ॥ *Subhāṣitaratnakośa* 784

110. aviraa-raï-keli-pasaṃga-sŏkkha-pabbhāra-īsi-kuṃṭhaïaṃ ı māṇa-ṇisāṇaa-ṇisiaṃ hoi puṇo ahiṇavaṃ pĕmmaṃ ॥ [avirata-rati-keli-prasaṅga-saukhya-prāgbhāra-iṣat-kuṇṭhitam ı māna-

niśānaka-niśitaṃ bhavati punaḥ abhinavaṃ prema ॥] *Līlāvaī* 1077

111. aṇṇa-mahilā-pasaṃgaṃ de dĕvva! karesu amha daïassa । purisā ĕkkaṃta-rasā ṇa hu dosa-guṇe viāṇaṃti ॥ [anya-mahilā-prasaṅgaṃ he deva! kuru asmākaṃ dayitasya । puruṣāḥ ekānta-rasāḥ na khalu doṣa-guṇān vijānanti ॥] *Gāhāsattasaī* 48

112. indīvareṇa nayanaṃ mukham ambujena kundena dantam adharaṃ navapallavena । aṅgāni campaka-dalaiḥ sa vidhāya vedhāḥ kānte! kathaṃ racitavān upalena cetaḥ ॥ *Daśarūpakāloka.* Commentary under Daśarūpaka 4.63, p. 131

113. ĕkka-saaṇammi sumuhī vimuhī garueṇa māṇa-baṃdheṇa । siviṇa-kalahammi hŏṃtī parammuhī sammuhī jāā ॥ [eka-śayane sumukhī vimukhī guruṇā māna-bandhena । svapna-kalahe bhavantī parāṅmukhī saṃmukhī jātā ॥] *Gāhāsattasaī* 911

114. sakhi! kalitaḥ skhalito ’yaṃ heyo naiva praṇāma-mātreṇa । ciram anubhavatu bhavatyā bāhu-latā-bandhanaṃ dhūrtaḥ ॥ *Subhāṣitaratnakośa* 672

115. adyāpi tan manasi samprati vartate me rātrau mayi kṣutavati kṣitipāla-putryā । “jīve” ti maṅgala-vacaḥ parihṛtya kopāt karṇe kṛtaṃ kanaka-pattram anālapantyā ॥ *Caurapañcāśikā* N11

116. kopaḥ tvayā yadi kṛto mayi paṅkajākṣi! so ’stu priyaḥ tava kim asti vidheyam anyat । āśleṣam arpaya mad-arpita-pūrvam uccair uccaiḥ samarpaya mad-arpita-cumbanaṃ ca ॥ *Subhāṣitaratnakośa* 671

117. svasti । amuka-sthānād amuko amuka-sthāne bhāryām amukāṃ sādaraṃ kuśalaṃ vārtayati yathā । kuśalam atrāsmākam। tatratya-samasta-mānuṣāṇāṃ kuśala-vārtā praheyā । anyat । tatra sthānād yaḥ ko ’py āgacchati sa sarvo gṛhasya rāvām eva karoti । yatrāpi vayaṃ na bhavāmaḥ tatrāpi kiñcin na bhavati । yad asmābhir māsa-dvitrāṇāṃ hetoḥ śambalaṃ muktaṃ tat tvayā dinair daśabhir aṣṭabhir eva niṣṭhāpitam । pade pade

vayaṃ dagdhāḥ tvayā । paraṃ tava doṣo nāsti । asmadīya-prāktana-janmanopārjita-doṣaḥ । yaduktam। pūrva-dattā tu yā vidyā pūrva-dattaṃ tu yad dhanam । pūrva-dattā tu yā nārī agre tiṣṭhati tiṣṭhati ॥ anyat । sarva-vārān yad vayaṃ bhaṇāmaḥ tat tat tvaṃ viparītaṃ karoṣi । kiṃ bahunā । yat tava kula-sadṛśaṃ tad anuṣṭheyam iti । *Lekhapaddhati.* 'Saroṣabhartṛbhāryālekho yathā', p. 64

118. gata-prāyā rātriḥ kṛśa-tanu! śaśī śīryata iva pradīpo 'yaṃ nidrā-vaśam upagato ghūrṇita iva । praṇāmānto mānaḥ tyajasi na tathāpi krudham aho kuca-pratyāsattyā hṛdayam api te caṇḍi! kaṭhinam ॥ *Prabandhacintāmaṇi* verse 109, p. 44

119. samāgatā hanta! tithir dvitīyā sakhi! dvitīyā dayiteva patyuḥ । yad etad-adhyāpana-magna-cetā na mām upetām api sandadhāti ॥ *Rasakalpadruma miśritaśṛṅgāravarṇana* 13

120. paṇaa-kuviāṇa dŏṇha vi alia-pasuttāṇa māṇaïllāṇa । ṇiccala-ṇiruddha-ṇīsāsa-diṇṇa-aṇṇāṇa ko mallo? ॥ [praṇaya-kupitayoḥ dvayor api alīka-prasuptayoḥ mānavatoḥ । niścala-niruddha-niḥśvāsa-datta-karṇayoḥ ko mallaḥ? ॥] *Gāhāsattasaī* 27

121. hastam ākṣipya yāto 'si balād iti kim adbhutam । hṛdayād yadi niryāsi pauruṣaṃ gaṇayāmi te ॥ *Subhāṣitāvalī* 1041

122. bhavatu viditaṃ vyarthālāpair alam priya! gamyatāṃ tanur api na te doṣo 'smākaṃ vidhiḥ tu parāṅmukhaḥ । tava yadi tathārūḍhaṃ prema prapannam imāṃ daśāṃ prakṛti-tarale kā naḥ pīḍā gate hata-jīvite ॥ *Amaruśataka* 30

123. pāa-paḍiassa païṇo puṭṭhiṃ putte samāruhaṃtammi । daḍha-maṇṇu-dūmiāi vi hāso ghariṇīa ṇikkaṃto ॥ [pāda-patitasya patyuḥ pṛṣṭhaṃ putre samāruhati । dṛḍha-manyu-dūnāyāḥ api hāso gṛhiṇyāḥ niṣkrāntaḥ ॥] *Gāhāsattasaī* 11

124. nīrasaṃ kāṣṭham evedaṃ satyaṃ te hṛdayaṃ yadi । tathāpi dīyatāṃ tasyai gatā sā daśamīṃ daśām ॥ *Saduktikarṇāmṛta* 627

125. dhūmāyate manasi mūrcchati ceṣṭiteṣu sandīpyate vapuṣi cakṣuṣi jājvalīti। vaktre parisphurati vāci vijṛmbhate 'syāḥ kāntāvamāna-janito bahumāna-vahniḥ ॥ *Saduktikarṇāmṛta* 694

126. uvvahaï daïa-gahiāharŏṭṭha-jhijjaṃta-rosa-paḍirāaṃ। pāṇosaraṃta-maïraṃ va phalia-casaaṃ imā vaaṇam ॥ [udvahati dayita-gṛhītādharoṣṭha-kṣīyamāṇa-roṣa-pratirāgaṃ pānāpasaran-madiram iva sphaṭika-caṣakam asyāḥ vadanam ॥] *Gauḍavaho* 690

127. aparādhād adhikaṃ māṃ vyathayati tava kapaṭa-vacana-racaneyam। śastrāghāto na tathā sūcī-vyadha-vedanā yādṛk ॥ *Āryāsaptaśatī* 11

128. kṛtvā vigraham āgato 'si niyataṃ nirvāsito vā tayā kāntalābha-vinodane kila vayaṃ viśrāma-bhūmiḥ tava। kiṃ nairāśya-nirutsukasya manasaḥ sandhukṣaṇair me punaḥ pītenātra kim auṣadhena kaṭunā susvāgataṃ gamyatām ॥ *Padmaprābhṛtaka* 3.40

129. ehijja so paüttho ahaaṃ kuppĕjja so vi aṇuṇĕjja। ia kassa vi phalaï maṇorahāṇa mālā piaamammi ॥ [eyāt sa proṣitaḥ ahaṃ kupyeyaṃ so 'pi anunayet। iti kasyāpi phalati manorathāṇāṃ mālā priyatame ॥] *Gāhāsattasaī* 17

130. kiṃ kāmī na kaca-grahair yam abalāḥ kliśnanti mattā balād yaṃ badhnanti na mekhalābhir athavā na ghnanti karṇotpalaiḥ। pakṣe tasya tu manmathaḥ sukṛtinaḥ tasyotsavo yauvanaṃ dāseneva rahasy apeta-vinayāḥ krīḍanti yenāṅganāḥ ॥ *Pādatāḍitaka* 1.30

131. prāsādīyati vaiṇavādi-gahanaṃ dīpīyati drāk tamaḥ paryaṅkīyati bhūtalaṃ dṛṣad api ślakṣṇopadhānīyati। kastūrīyati kardamaḥ kim aparaṃ? yūno rasāviṣṭayor yenālokitayoḥ sa vandya-mahimā devo namasyaḥ smaraḥ ॥ *Subhāṣitaratnabhāṇḍāgāra manasijapraśaṃsā* 22

132. āṇā-saāi dĕṃtī taha surae harisa-viasia-kavolā। gose vi oṇaa-muhī aha sĕ tti piaṃ ṇa saddhahimo ॥ [ājñā-śatāni dadatī tathā

surate harṣa-vikasita-kapolā। prātar api avanata-mukhī iyaṃ sā iti priyāṃ na śraddadhmaḥ॥] *Gāhāsattasaī* 23

133. niṣpiṣyāhi-phaṇā-maṇīn sarabhasaṃ santīrya tāḥ tā nadīḥ krāntvā kaṇṭaka-saṅkaṭāṃ ca padavīṃ dhvānte ghane varṣati। talpopāntam upetya hanta! vanitā kenāpy aho hetunā śayyāyāḥ tv adhirohaṇe priya-karālambaṃ kilāpekṣate॥ *Vidyākarasahasraka* 422

134. bālāyā nava-saṃgame nipuṇatāṃ prekṣyānyathāśaṅkino bhartuḥ cittam avekṣya paṅkajamukhī tat-pārśva-kuddye 'likhat। ekaṃ bhadra-mataṅgajaṃ tadupari krodhāt patantaṃ śiśuṃ siṃhī-garbha-viniḥsṛtārdha-vapuṣaṃ dṛṣṭvā sa hṛṣṭo 'bhavat॥ *Anyoktimuktāvalī* 2.21

135. gĕṇhaï kaṃṭhammi balā cuṃbaï ṇaaṇāi haraï me siaaṃ। paḍhama-suraammi raaṇī varassa emea bolei॥ [gṛhṇāti kaṇṭhe balāt cumbati nayane harati me sicayam। prathama-surate rajanī varasya evam eva vyatikrāmati॥] *Śṛṅgāraprakāśa* 12.3, Vol. 2, p. 1103

136. ṇa vi taha paḍhama-samāgama-suraa-suhe pāvie vi parioso। jaha vīa-diaha-savilakkha-lakkhie vaaṇa-kamalammi॥ [nāpi tathā prathama-samāgama-surata-sukhe prāpte 'pi paritoṣaḥ। yathā dvitīya-divasa-savilakṣa-lakṣite vadana-kamale॥] *Gāhāsattasaī* 209

137. prathamaṃ praveśitā yā vāsāgāraṃ kathañcana sakhībhiḥ। na śṛṇotīva prātaḥ sā nirgamanasya saṅketam॥ *Āryāsaptaśatī* 385

138. sohaï jaha malia-pasāhaṇālaaṃ kāmiṇīṇa gosammi। vaaṇaṃ savvāara-viraïaṃ pi ṇa tahā ṇisāraṃbhe॥ [śobhate yathā mṛdita-prasādhanālakaṃ kāminīnām prataḥ। vadanaṃ sarvādara-viracitam api na tathā niśārambhe॥] *Līlāvaī* 1099

139. indrāya vīkṣamāṇaḥ tan-mukham āsvādayann anantāya। spṛhayāmi cādya dayitām āliṅge kārtavīryāya॥ *Subhāṣitasudhānidhi* 232.2

140. cumbijjai saa-huttaṃ avaruṃḍijjai sahassa-huttaṃ pi ı ramia puṇo vi ramijjai pie jaṇe ṇatthi puṇaruttaṃ ıı [cumbyate śatakṛtvaḥ āliṅgyate sahasra-kṛtvaḥ api ı rantvā punar api ramyate priye jane nāsti punaruktam ıı] *Dhvanyāloka* 1.17, p. 62. The text presented here is V.M. Kulkarni's restoration.

141. paripatati payonidhau pataṅgaḥ sarasiruhām udareṣu matta-bhṛṅgaḥ ı upavana-taru-koṭare vihaṅgo yuvati-janeṣu śanaiḥ śanair anaṅgaḥ ıı *Bhojaprabandha* 161, p. 34

142. svinnaṃ maṇḍalam aindavaṃ vilulitaṃ srag-bhāra-naddhaṃ tamaḥ prāg eva prathamāna-kaitaka-śikhā-līlāyitaṃ susmitam ı śāntaṃ kuṇḍala-tāṇḍavaṃ kuvalaya-dvandvaṃ tiromīlitaṃ vītaṃ vidruma-sītkṛtaṃ na hi tato jāne kim āsīd iti ıı *Bhojaprabandha* 252, p. 56

143. jāti-svabhāva-guṇa-deśaja-dharma-ceṣṭā bhāveṅgiteṣu vikalo rati-tantra-mūḍhaḥ ı labdhvāpi hi skhalati yauvanam aṅganānāṃ kiṃ nārikela-phalam āpya kapiḥ karoti? ıı *Ratirahasya* 7

144. śāstrāṇāṃ viṣayaḥ tāvad yāvan manda-rasā narāḥ ı rati-cakre pravṛtte tu naiva śāstraṃ na ca kramaḥ ıı *Kāmasūtra* 2.2.32

145. mugdhe! tavāsmi dayitā puruṣo bhava tvam ity uktayā "nahi nahī" ti śiro 'vadhūya ı svasmāt karāt priya-kare valayaṃ kṣipantyā vācaṃ vinābhyupagamaḥ kathito mṛgākṣyā ıı *Subhāṣitasudhānidhi* 35.2

146. taiḥ taiḥ cāṭubhir ājñayā kila tadā vṛtte rati-vyatyaye lajjā-mantharayā tayā nivasite bhrāntyā madīye 'ṃśuke ı tat-paṭṭāṃśukam udvahann aham api smitvā yad ukto "dhunā veṣo yujyata eṣa eva hi tave" ty etan na vismaryate ıı *Sūktimuktāvalī* 43.17

147. avidheyam anākhyeyam pravicāryaṃ chādanīyam aviṣahyaṃ ı na babhūva tayoḥ tasminn āviddhārabdha-surata-saṃmarde ıı *Kuṭṭanīmata* 383

148. dhairyasya yad anāyattaṃ lajjāyā yad agocaraḥ । yad ayuktaṃ vicārasya tad abhūt surataṃ tayoḥ ॥ *Subhāṣitasudhānidhi* 34.1

149. jaṃ jaṃ so ṇijjhāaï aṃgoāsaṃ mahaṃ aṇimisaccho । pacchāemi a taṃ taṃ icchāmi a teṇa dīsaṃtaṃ ॥ [yaṃ yaṃ sa nirdhyāyati aṅgāvakāśaṃ mamānimiṣākṣaḥ । pracchādayāmi ca taṃ tam icchāmi ca tena dṛśyamānam ॥] *Gāhāsattasaī* 73

150. jāo so vi vilakkho mae vi hasiūṇa gāḍham uvaūḍho । paḍhamosariassa ṇiaṃsaṇassa gaṃṭhiṃ vimaggaṃto ॥ [jātaḥ so 'pi vilakṣaḥ mayāpi hasitvā gāḍham upagūḍhaḥ । prathamāpasṛtasya nivasanasya granthiṃ vimārgayamāṇaḥ ॥] *Gāhāsattasaī* 351

151. nādhanyān viparīta-mohana-rasa-preṅkhan-nitamba-sthalī-lolad-bhūṣaṇa-kiṅkiṇī-kalarava-vyāmiśra-kaṇṭha-svanam । saṃrambha-ślatha-keśabandha-vigalan-muktākalāpa-druta-śvāsa-ccheda-taraṅgita-stana-yugaṃ prīṇāti śṛṅgāriṇī ॥ *Subhāṣitāvalī* 581

152. candujjoeṇa mao maeṇa candāavo ṇu vaḍḍhia-pasaro । dohi vi tehi ṇu maaṇo maaṇeṇa ṇu do vi te ṇiā aï-bhūmiṃ ॥ [candroddyotena madaḥ madena candrātapaḥ nu vardhita-prasaraḥ । dvābhyām api tābhyāṃ nu madanaḥ madanena nu dvau api tau nītau atibhūmim ॥] *Rāvaṇavaho* 10.81

153. atra brūmo yat tāvat prathama-samāgame rataṃ tad apy alabdha-visrambhāyāṃ kāminyām ajñāta-gādham iva saraḥ śaṅkāvagāhaṃ bhavati । *Dhūrtaviṭasaṃvāda* near 4.120 p. 373

154. "tvarasva kānte" ti bhayād bravīti yaṃ kāminī corita-samprayogā । krītāḥ tayā tasya bhavanti puṃsaḥ prāṇā yatheṣṭaṃ parikalpya mūlyam ॥ *Dhūrtaviṭasaṃvāda* 4.135

155. ye ca praṇaya-kupitāsu kāminīṣu tat-kālotkaṇṭhānurūpa-ramyān prasādanopāyān mitraiḥ saha cintayataḥ sāyāmā iva divasā vrajanti kutaḥ te īrṣyā-virahite svarge? yac ca bhāva-niviṣṭāṅgyo vakṣaḥsthala-śāyinyo bakula-kusuma-niḥśvāsa-mārutair ghrāṇam āghrāpayantyaḥ striyo nidrā-sukham

utpādayanti kutaḥ tan nidrā-virahite svarge? yāni vāruṇī-mada-vilulitākṣarāṇi kim api lajjāvanti priyāṇi priyārthāni vacāṃsi strīṇāṃ kutaḥ tāni pāna-virahite svarge? sukṛta-sītkārāṇi śvasita-bahulāny upagūhana-dūtāni nava-vadhū-ratāni kuta eva svarge? bho māṃ prati varaṃ śrotriyair vṛddhaiḥ sahāsituṃ nāpsarobhiḥ! tāḥ tu dīrghāyuṣmatyaḥ saṃskṛta-bhāṣiṇyo mahā-prabhāvāḥ ca śrūyante। yāsu vasiṣṭhāgastya-prabhṛtayo maharṣayaḥ samutpannāḥ tāsu ko visrambhaḥ? *Dhūrtaviṭasaṃvāda* 4.165 p. 409

156. mālatī śirasi jṛmbhaṇonmukhī candanaṃ vapuṣi kuṅkumāvilam । vakṣasi priyatamā madālasā svarga eṣa pariśiṣṭa āgamaḥ ॥ *Śatakatraya* 116

157. muhur aviśadā viśrambhārdrā muhuḥ smṛta-manyavo muhur asaralāḥ prema-prahvā muhur muhur asthirāḥ । vitatha-śapathopālambhājñā muhur madhurā muhuḥ parivavṛdhire niṣparyantā mitho mithunoktayaḥ ॥ *Kapphiṇābhyudaya* 14.12

158. āśleṣa-śeṣā ratir aṅganānām āmoda-śeṣā kuca-kuṅkuma-śrīḥ । tūṇīra-śeṣaḥ kusumāyudho 'pi pratyūṣa-śeṣā rajanī babhūva ॥ *Rasikajīvana* 7.122

159. gāhāṇa a geāṇa a tantī-saddāṇa poḍha-mahilāṇa । tāṇaṃ sŏ ccia daṇḍo je tāṇa rasaṃ ṇa āṇaṃti ॥ [gāthānāṃ ca geyānāṃ ca tantrī-śabdānāṃ prauḍha-mahilānām । teṣām sa eva daṇḍaḥ ye teṣāṃ rasaṃ na jānanti ॥] *Gāhāsattasaī* 815

160. ālāne gṛhyate hastī vājī valgāsu gṛhyate । hṛdaye gṛhyate nārī yadīdaṃ nāsti gamyatām ॥ *Mṛcchakaṭika* 1.50

161. ayi! nakhāṅkita-lāñchita-pustike! tvam asi mama jīvitavairiṇī (?) । tvayi niveśita-niścala-buddhinā yad amunā paśunā vayam ujjhitāḥ ॥ *Kāmasamūha* 367

162. avvo! tahiṃ tahiṃ ciya gayaṇaṃ bhamiūṇa vīsamaṃteṇa । bohittha-vāyaseṇa va hasāviyā daḍḍha-pĕmmeṇa ॥ [aho tatra tatraiva gaganaṃ bhrāntvā viśrāmyatā । vahitra-vāyaseneva hāsitāḥ dagdha-premṇā ॥] *Vajjālagga* 344

163. tṛṣitāṃ hariṇīṃ hariṇaḥ tṛṣitaṃ hariṇaṃ vijānatī hariṇī ı mitam ambu palvalasthaṃ kapaṭaṃ pibataḥ parasparālokam ıı *Rasakalpadruma* p. 179

164. nātheti paruṣam ucitaṃ priyeti dāsety anugraho yatra ı tad dāmpatyam ito 'nyan nārī rajjuḥ paśuḥ puruṣaḥ ıı *Āryāsaptaśatī* 336

165. jaṃ dosesu nisammai jaṃ uvaesehĩ tīrae caliuṃ ı jaṃ ca sahae vioyaṃ taṃ sahi! pimmaṃ ciya na hoi ıı [yad doṣeṣu niśāmyati yad upadeśaiḥ śakyate calitum ı yac ca sahate viyogaṃ tat sakhi! premaiva na bhavati ıı] *Gāhārayaṇakoso* 415

166. mayānuyujyamāneyaṃ kim ivodīrayiṣyati? ı iti śaṅkākulaḥ praṣṭum icchāmi ca bibhemi ca ıı *Kādambarīkalyāṇanāṭaka* 7.13

167. anargala-pravāhasya payaso 'sti gati-kramaḥ ı ruddhasya bandha-vicchede kaḥ kramo 'sya vinirgame? ıı yaḥ sarvadaiva viṣayeṣu viṣakta-cittaḥ tasya krameṇa madanaḥ kurute vikārān ı strī-kāmanā yadi sadā niyatasya jātu tatra kramo 'sti kim anaṅga-parākramāṇām? ıı *Kuśakumudvatīyanāṭaka* 2.13–14

168. tauryaṃ dīpa-samindhanaṃ smṛti-pathāl lupyeta sūryodaye ratna-svarṇa-vibhūṣaṇādi na-cirād gacchet karaṃ śāsituḥ ı artho jātu bhajed anartha-padavīṃ jīryed dukūlādikaṃ gārhasthyopaniṣat paraṃ yad uta vāṃ tiṣṭhed guṇānāṃ gaṇaḥ ıı *Kaṇṭakāñjali* 142

169. sauvarṇaḥ cheda-nigharṣa-tāpaiḥ tulya-ruciḥ sadā ı mṛjyamānasya vaimalyaṃ tāmra-saṃjñasya nānyathā ıı rīti-nāmnaḥ tu mālinyaṃ snehenāpy upajāyate ı saisasyādau ca madhye ca kṣaye ca malinā ruciḥ ıı tīkṣṇa-svabhāvāl lohasya kāṭhinyāc ca na namratā ı maṇināmā ca nirvyājaḥ sahaja-svaccha-niścalaḥ ıı svabhāva-bhiduraḥ kāca-saṃjñaḥ chala-nirīkṣakaḥ ı śailo 'pi gaurava-sthāyī hṛdayābhāva-nīrasaḥ ıı *Samayamātṛkā* 5.23–26

170. tvat-kṛte yānayā yātanānubhūtā, sā yadi nabhaḥ pattrāyate, sāgaro melānandāyate, brahmā lipikārāyate, bhujaga-patir vā kathakāyate, tadā kimapi katham apy anekair yuga-sahasrair abhilikhyate kathyate vā । *Vāsavadattā* pp. 306–07

171. saha-jaggirāṇa saha-sovirāṇa saha-harisa-soyavantāṇa । nayaṇāṇa va dhannāṇaṃ ājammam akittimaṃ pimmaṃ ॥ [saha-jāgaritṝṇāṃ saha-svapitṝṇāṃ saha-harṣa-śokavatām । nayanānām iva dhanyānām ājanma akṛtrimaṃ prema ॥] *Mallikāmakarandanāṭaka* 6.6

172. īsāluo paī se rattiṃ mahuaṃ ṇa dei ucceuṃ । uccei appaṇa ccia māe aï-ujjua-sahāo ॥ [īrṣyāluḥ patiḥ tasyāḥ rātriṃ madhūkāni na dadāty uccetum । uccinoti ātmanaiva mātaḥ! ati-ṛju-svabhāvaḥ ॥] *Gāhāsattasaī* 159

173. jaṃ keaveṇa pĕmmaṃ jaṃ ca valā jaṃ ca attha-loheṇa । jaṃ uvaroha-ṇimittaṃ ṇamo ṇamo tassa pĕmmassa ॥ [yat kaitavena prema yac ca balāt yac ca artha-lobhena । yad uparodha-nimittaṃ namo namaḥ tasmai premṇe ॥] *Gāhāsattasaī* 744

174. imāṃ khanāmy oṣadhiṃ vīrudham balavattamām । yayā sapatnīm bādhate yayā saṃvindate patim ॥ uttānaparṇe subhage devajūte sahasvati । sapatnīm me parā dhama patim me kevalaṃ kuru ॥ upa te ’dhāṃ sahamānām abhi tvādhāṃ sahīyasā । mām anu pra te mano vatsaṃ gaur iva dhāvatu pathā vār iva dhāvatu ॥ *Ṛgveda* 10.145.01,10.145.02,10.145.06

175. jattha ṇa ujjāgarao jattha ṇa īsā visūraṇaṃ māṇo । sabbhāva-cāḍuaṃ jattha ṇa tthi ṇeho tahiṃ ṇa tthi ॥ [yatra na ujjāgaraḥ yatra na īrṣyā khedaḥ mānaḥ । sadbhāva-cāṭukaṃ yatra nāsti snehaḥ tatra nāsti ॥] *Gāhāsattasaī* 829

176. jāe māṇa-ppasare phiṭṭe nehe gayammi sabbhāve । abbhatthaṇāi pĕmmaṃ kīraṃtaṃ kerisaṃ hoi? ॥ [yāte māna-prasare bhraṣṭe snehe gate sadbhāve । abhyarthanayā prema kriyamāṇaṃ kīdṛśaṃ bhavati? ॥] *Vajjālagga* 344

177. pĕmmassa virohia-saṃdhiassa paccakkha-diṭṭha-viliassa ı uaassa va tāvia-sīalassa viraso raso hoi ıı [premṇaḥ virodhita-sandhitasya pratyakṣa-dṛṣṭa-vyalīkasya ı udakasyeva tāpita-śītalasya viraso raso bhavati ıı] *Gāhāsattasaī* 53

178. unmatta-prema-saṃrambhād ārabhante yad aṅganāḥ ı tatra pratyūham ādhātuṃ brahmāpi khalu kātaraḥ ıı *Śatakatraya* 115

179. etat sarvaṃ śṛṇuta vacanaṃ saṅgrahād atra sakhyaḥ! prāṇānāṃ naḥ phalam avikalaṃ nūnam eṣā sakhī vaḥ ı viśleṣe 'smin pracalati bhṛśaṃ dīpikeva pravāte satyām asyāṃ vayam atamasaḥ sarvathā rakṣatainām ıı *Sūktimuktāvalī* 131.13

180. ṇeho kahavi ṇa kīraï ahavā kīraï ratta-kaṃbala-sarittho ı aṇavarayaṃ dhoyamāṇo aṇṇaṃ vaṇṇaṃ ṇa giṇhei ıı [snehaḥ katham api na kriyate athavā kriyate rakta-kambala-sadṛśaḥ ı anavaratam kṣālyamānaḥ anyaṃ varṇam na gṛhṇāti ıı] (metrically defective) *Rasāulagāhākosa* (Folio 6 verso, line 9).

181. gāmāruha mhi gāme vasāmi ṇaaraṭṭhiiṃ ṇa āṇāmi ı ṇāariāṇaṃ païṇo haremi jā homi sā homi ıı [grāmīṇā asmi grāme vasāmi nagara-sthitiṃ na jānāmi ı nāgarikāṇāṃ patīn harāmi yā bhavāmi sā bhavāmi ıı] *Gāhāsattasaī* 705

182. gataḥ pūrvo yāmaḥ śruti-virasayā malla-kathayā dvitīyo vikṣiptaḥ palalaguḍa-bāhya-vyatikaraiḥ ı tṛtīyo gātrāṇām upacaya-kathābhir vigalitaḥ tataḥ tan nirvṛttaṃ kathayitum alam tvayy api yadi ıı *Pādatāḍitaka* 1.190

183. salilŏlla-dāruāï va aṃtŏ ccia simisimāamāṇāiṃ ı maaṇāṇaleṇa lajjāluāṇā ḍajjhaṃti hiaāiṃ ıı [salilārdra-dārukāṇīva antar eva simasimāyamānāni ı madanānalena lajjālūnāṃ dahyante hṛdayāni ıı] *Śṛṅgāraprakāśa* 12.209, Vol. 2, p. 1139

184. kiṃ dāva kaā ahavā karesi kāhisi a suhaa! ĕttāhe ı avarāhāṇa alajjira! sāhasu kaarā khamijjaṃti ıı [kiṃ tāvat kṛtā athavā karoṣi kariṣyasi ca subhaga! idānīm ı aparādhānāṃ nirlajja! śādhi katare kṣamyante ıı] *Gāhāsattasaī* 90

185. ākāreṇa śaśī girā parabhṛtaḥ pārāvataḥ cumbane haṃsaḥ caṅkramaṇe samaṃ dayitayā ratyā vimarde gajaḥ ı itthaṃ bhartari me samasta-yuvati-ślāghyair guṇaiḥ sevite kṣuṇṇaṃ nāsti vivāhitaḥ patir iti syān naiṣa doṣo yadi ıı *Subhāṣitāvalī* 2386

186. subhagaṃ vadati janaḥ taṃ nija-patir iti naiṣa rocate mahyam ı pīyūṣe 'pi hi bheṣaja-bhāvopanate bhavaty aruciḥ ıı *Āryāsaptaśatī* 671

187. subhagam-manyena ca mayā sva-dhanasya sva-gṛhasya sva-gaṇasya sva-dehasya sva-jīvitasya ca saiveśvarīkṛtā ı kṛtaḥ cāham anayā mala-mallaka-śeṣaḥ ı *Daśakumāracarita* 7.67

188. taïā maha gaṃḍa-tthala-ṇimiaṃ diṭṭhiṃ ṇa ṇesi aṇṇatto ı ĕṇhiṃ sa ccea ahaṃ te a kavolā ṇa sā diṭṭhī ıı [tadā mama gaṇḍa-sthala-nyastāṃ dṛṣṭiṃ na nayasi anyataḥ ı idānīṃ sā eva ahaṃ tau ca kapolau na sā dṛṣṭiḥ ıı] *Gāhāsattasaī* 939

189. kāle māṣaṃ sasye māsaṃ vadati śakāsaṃ yaḥ ca sakāśam ı uṣṭre lumpati śaṃ vā raṃ vā tasmai dattā vikaṭanitambā ıı *Kāvyālaṅkāraṭippaṇī* 7.47

190. āsasa muddhe! āsasa caḍulaṃ saṃkamaï aṇṇamaṇṇesu ı viṃjhagiri-sela-sihare vāṇara-līlaṃ vahaï pĕmmaṃ ıı [āśvasihi mugdhe! āśvasihi caṭulaṃ saṅkramate anyeṣv anyeṣu ı vindhyagiri-śaila-śikhare vānara-līlāṃ vahati prema ıı] *Kuvalayamālā* Part 1, p. 265

191. jaṃ jaṃ te ṇa suhāaï taṃ taṃ ṇa karemi jaṃ mamāattaṃ ı ahaaṃ cia jaṃ ṇa suhāmi suhaa! taṃ kiṃ mamāattaṃ? ıı [yat yat te na sukhāyate tat tan na karomi yan mamāyattam ı aham eva yan na sukhayāmi subhaga! tat kim mamāyattam? ıı] *Gāhāsattasaī* 617

192. mama prema tavaudāsyaṃ spardhayā vardhitaṃ mithaḥ ı jetavyam anayoḥ kena na jāne paṅkajānane! ıı *Rasakalpadruma* 33, p. 138

193. paryastālaka-gaṇḍa-pāli vadanāmbhojaṃ mayā cumbitaṃ pratyaṅgaṃ kara-pallavena pulaka-śreṇī-spṛśā lālitam ।
dorbhyāṃ tasya kaṭhora-kaṅkaṇa-ravaṃ dor-vallir āliṅgitā nidrāty eva muhuḥ tathāpi dayitaḥ kasmai kim ācakṣmahe? ॥
Padyaracanā 450

194. ḍacchanti jāṇa ṇāmeṇa kāa-kāāri-pakkha-piñchāi । paṇaya-parūḍhaṃ pi khaṇeṇa tāṇa pĕmmaṃ visaṃghaḍai ॥ [dahyante yayor nāmnā kāka-kākāri-pakṣa-piñchāni । praṇaya-prarūḍham api kṣaṇena tayoḥ prema visaṅghaṭate ॥] *Haramekhalā* 2.49

195. yathā kāṣṭhaṃ ca kāṣṭhaṃ ca sameyātāṃ mahodadhau । sametya ca vyatīyātāṃ tadvad bhūta-samāgamaḥ ॥ *Mahābhārata* 12.28.36

196. "idaṃ kṛṣṇaṃ" "kṛṣṇaṃ" "priyatama! nanu śvetam" "atha kiṃ" "gamiṣyāmo "yāmo" "bhavatu gamanen""ātha bhavatu" । purā yenaivaṃ me ciram anusṛtā citta-padavī sa evānyo jātaḥ sakhi! paricitāḥ kasya puruṣāḥ ॥ *Subhāṣitāvalī* 1138

197. sama-sŏkkha-dukkha-parivaḍḍhiāṇa kāleṇa rūḍha-pĕmmāṇa । mihuṇāṇa maraï jaṃ taṃ khu jiaï iaraṃ muaṃ hoi ॥ [sama-saukhya-duḥkha-parivardhitayoḥ kālena rūḍha-premṇoḥ । mithunayoḥ mriyate yat tat khalu jīvati itaran mṛtaṃ bhavati ॥] *Gāhāsattasaī* 142

198. avvo! kālassa gaī so vi juā sarasa-kavva-dullalio । paḍhaï parāsara-saddaṃ amhe vi ṇiaṃ païṃ gamimo ॥ [aho! kālasya gatiḥ so 'pi yuvā sarasa-kāvya-durlalitaḥ । paṭhati parāśara-śabdaṃ vayam api nijaṃ patiṃ gacchāmaḥ ॥] *Gāhāsattasaī* 892

199. "kathaṃ mayaṃ, bhante! mātugāme paṭipajjāmā?" ti । "adassanaṃ, ānandā!" ti । "dassane bhagavā! sati kathaṃ paṭipajjitabban?" ti । "anālāpo ānandā!" ti । "ālapantena pana bhante!, kathaṃ paṭipajjitabban?" ti । "sati, ānanda!, upaṭṭhāpetabbā" ti । ["kathaṃ vayaṃ bhagavan! mātṛgrāme pratipadyemahi?" iti । "adarśanam ānanda!"

iti । "darśane bhagavan! sati kathaṃ pratipattavyaṃ?" iti । "anālāpaḥ ānanda!" īti । "ālapatā punar bhagavan! kathaṃ pratipattavyam?" iti । "smṛtiḥ ānanda! upasthāpayitavyā" iti ।] *Mahāparinibbānasutta* D. xvi.5.11, p. 141

200. tathābhūd asmākaṃ prathamam avibhinnā tanur iyaṃ tato nu tvaṃ preyān aham api hatāśā priyatamā । idānīṃ nāthaḥ tvaṃ vayam api kalatraṃ kim aparaṃ mayāptaṃ prāṇānāṃ kuliśa-kaṭhinānāṃ phalam idam ॥ *Subhāṣitaratnakośa* 646

201. sākṣi-nikocaṃ sakhyāḥ pāṇi-talaṃ pāṇinā samāhatya । yaṃ naram upahasati strī dadātu tasmai mahī randhram ॥ *Kuṭṭanīmata* 632

202. "mā yāhī" ty apamaṅgalaṃ "vraja" kila snehena śūnyaṃ vacaḥ "tiṣṭhe" ti prabhutā "yathāruci kuruṣv" aiṣāpy udāsīnatā । "no jīvāmi vinā tvaye" ti vacanaṃ sambhāvyate vā na vā tan mām śikṣaya nātha! yat samucitaṃ vaktuṃ tvayi prasthite ॥ *Subhāṣitāvalī* 1049

203. yūyaṃ vayaṃ vayaṃ yūyam ity āsīn matir āvayoḥ । kim jātam adhunā yena yūyaṃ yūyaṃ vayaṃ vayam? ॥ *Śatakatraya* 312

204. adyāpi hi nṛśamsasya pituḥ te divaso gataḥ । tamasā pihitaḥ panthāḥ ehi putraka! śevahe ॥ *Subhāṣitāvalī* 1106

205. jo sīsammi viiṇṇo majjha juāṇehi gaṇavaī āsi । taṃ cia ĕṇhiṃ paṇamāmi haa-jare! hohi saṃtuṭṭhā ॥ [yaḥ śirasi vitīrṇaḥ mama yuvabhiḥ ganapatiḥ āsīt । tam eva idānīṃ praṇamāmi hata-jare! bhava santuṣṭā ॥] *Gāhāsattasaī* 372

206. sakhe puṇḍarīka, suviditam etan mama। kevalam idam eva pṛcchāmi, yad etad ārabdhaṃ bhavatā kim idaṃ gurubhir upadiṣṭam, uta dharma-śāstreṣu paṭhitam, uta dharmārjanopāyo 'yam, utāparaḥ tapasāṃ prakāraḥ, uta svarga-gamana-mārgo 'yam, uta vrata-rahasyam idam, uta mokṣa-prāpti-yuktir iyam, āhosvid anyo niyama-prakāraḥ? katham etad yuktaṃ bhavato manasāpi cintayitum, kiṃ punar ākhyātum īkṣituṃ vā। aprabuddha ivānena

manmatha-hatakenopahāsāspadatāṃ nīyamānam ātmānaṃ nāvabudhyase । mūḍho hi madanenāyāsyate । kā vā sukhāśā sādhu-jana-ninditeṣv evaṃvidheṣu prākṛta-jana-bahumateṣu viṣayeṣu bhavataḥ । sa khalu dharmabuddhyā viṣalatāṃ siñcati, kuvalayamāleti nistriṃśalatām āliṅgati, kṛṣṇāguru-dhūmalekheti kṛṣṇa-sarpam avagūhati, ratnam iti jvalantam aṅgāram abhispṛśati, mṛṇālam iti duṣṭa-vāraṇa-danta-musalam unmūlayati, mūḍho viṣayopabhogeṣv aniṣṭānubandhiṣu yaḥ sukhabuddhim āropayati। adhigata-viṣaya-tattvo 'pi kasmāt khadyota iva jyotir nivāryam idaṃ jñānam udvahasi, yato na nivārayasi prabala-rajaḥ-prasara-kaluṣitāni srotāṃsīvonmārga-prasthitānīndriyāṇi, na niyamayasi vā kṣubhitaṃ manaḥ । ko 'yam anaṅgo nāma । dhairyam avalambya nirbhartsyatām ayaṃ durācāraḥ। *Kādambarī pūrvabhāga*, p. 330–31

207. kaïava-rahiaṃ pĕmmaṃ ṇa tthi ccia māmi! māṇuse loe । aha hoi kassa viraho virahe hŏṃtammi ko jiaï? ॥ [kaitava-rahitaṃ prema nāsti eva māmi! mānuṣe loke । atha bhavati kasya virahaḥ virahe sati ko jīvati? ॥] *Gāhāsattasaī* 124

208. snehena kaścin na samo 'sti pāśaḥ sroto na tṛṣṇā-samam asti hāri । rāgāgninā nāsti samaḥ tathāgniḥ tac cet trayaṃ nāsti sukhaṃ ca te 'sti ॥ *Saundarānanda* 102

209. dampatyoḥ pākṣikāt premṇaḥ premābhāvaḥ sukhāvahaḥ । eka-karṇastha-tāḍaṅkād atāḍaṅkaṃ mukhaṃ varam ॥ *Sūktimuktāvalī* 88.11

210. eko rāgiṣu rājate priyatamā-dehārdha-hārī haro nīrāgeṣu jino vimukta-lalanā-saṅgo na yasmāt paraḥ । durvāra-smara-bāṇa-pannaga-viṣa-vyāsaṅga-mugdho janaḥ śeṣaḥ kāma-viḍambito hi viṣayān bhoktuṃ na moktuṃ kṣamaḥ ॥ *Śatakatraya* 224

211. dalati hṛdayaṃ gāḍhodvegaṃ dvidhā na tu bhidyate vahati vikalaḥ kāyo mūrcchāṃ na muñcati cetanām । jvalayati tanūm antar-dāhaḥ karoti na bhasmasāt praharati vidhir marma-cchedī na kṛntati jīvitam ॥ *Mālatīmādhava* 9.11

212. he bahmaṇa! mā sirajasi sirajasi mā desi māṇusaṃ jammaṃ । aha jammaṃ mā pimmaṃ aha pimmaṃ mā viyogaṃ ca ॥ [he brahman! mā sṛja sṛjasi mā dehi mānuṣaṃ janma । atha janma mā prema atha prema mā viyogaṃ ca ॥] *Mādhavānalākhyāna* 140

213. jammaṃtara-lakkha-parūḍha-dukkha-rukkhassa tinni sāhāo । sevā khalesu vihavo paresu pimmaṃ apimmesu ॥ [janmāntara-lakṣa-prarūḍha-duḥkha-vṛkṣasya tisraḥ śākhāḥ । sevā khaleṣu vibhavaḥ pareṣu prema apremasu ॥] *Mallikāmakarandanāṭaka* 5

214. jīaṃ jala-biṃdu-samaṃ saṃpattīo taraṃga-lolāo । sumiṇaya-samaṃ ca pimmaṃ jaṃ jāṇasu taṃ karijjāsu ॥ [jīvo jala-bindu-samaḥ sampattayaḥ taraṅga-lolāḥ । svapna-samaṃ ca prema yat jānīhi tat kuryāḥ ॥] *Subhāsiapajjasaṃgaha* 133

215. desuccāḍaṇu sihi-kaḍhaṇu ghaṇa-kuṭṭaṇu jaṃ loi । maṃjiṭṭhaĕ ai-rattiaĕ savvu sahĕvvaü hoi ॥ [deśoccāṭanaṃ śikhi-kvathanaṃ ghana-kuṭṭanam yat loke । mañjiṣṭhāyāḥ ati-raktāyāḥ sarvaṃ soḍhavyaṃ bhavati ॥] *Siddhahemaśabdānuśāsana* 438 p. 102

216. puṣpeṣuṃ smara satkuruṣva nama vā gālyā samabhyukṣa vā chetsyan nirbhaya-pāṇir ādhi-śatakaṃ prādurbhaved vā na vā । kumbhīdāsati tasya tu smara-rasaḥ prācāṃ ya īṣṭe girāṃ moghair naḥ kimu daivatair? akaruṇo hiṃsrair asau bhakṣyatām ॥ suhāsasya

217. svar-loka-vāra-taruṇī-taruṇa-pradāni kūpe kuru smṛti-purāṇa-nideśanāni । atraiva pustakam idaṃ paṭhataḥ śubhāni kroḍe tava pratiphalanti phalāni tāni ॥ suhāsasya

218. durvṛttāḥ vidadhatu māpasavyataḥ tvāṃ preyasyo dṛḍhataram ālagantu kaṇṭhe । dṛṣṭir mā nipatatu sa-spaśā gurūṇāṃ sandhattām aniśam iṣu-dvayīm anaṅgaḥ ॥ suhāsasya

- iti karṇāṭābhijanābhyāṃ turantura-nagara-vāstavyābhyāṃ dampatibhyām anūṣā-suhāsābhyāṃ viracito 'yam śṛṅgāra-padya-saṅgrahaḥ samāptaḥ । śivam astu sarvajagataḥ ॥

Primary Sources

1. *Allegorical Pearls* of Haṃsavijaya Gaṇi: *Haṃsavijayagaṇisamuccitā Anyoktimuktāvalī*. Edited by Pandit Kedārnātha and Wāsudeva Laxmaṇ Shāstrī Paṇashīkar. Bombay: Nirnaya Sagar, 1907.
2. *Amaru's Hundred (Amaruśataka)* of Amaru: *Amaruśataka*. Edited by Pandit Durgāprasāda and Vāsudeva Laxmaṇ Śāstrī Paṇaśīkar. Bombay: Nirnaya Sagar, 1916.
3. *Ambrosia for the Ears (Saduktikarṇāmṛta)* of Śrīdharadāsa: *Sadukti-Karnāmrta of Sridharadāsa*. Edited by Sures Chandra Banerji. Calcutta: Firma K.L. Mukhopadhyay, 1965.
4. *Ambrosial Ocean of Verse (Subhāṣitasudhānidhi)* of Sāyaṇa: *Sāyaṇa's Subhāṣita-Sudhānidhi (An Anthology)*. Edited by K. Krishnamoorthy. Dharwar: Karnatak University, 1968.
5. *Apabhramsha Grammar (Siddhahemaśabdānuśāsana)* of Hemacandra: *Apabhraṃśa Vyākaraṇa: Vistṛta Bhūmikā, Śabdārtha, Chāyā, Anuvāda, Ṭippana, Aura Śabdasūcī Sahita*. Edited by Harivallabha Bhāyāṇī. Translated by Bindu Bhaṭṭa.

Ahamadabada: Kalikāla sarvajña śrī hemacandrācārya navama janmaśatābdī śmrti saṃskāra śikṣanavidhi, 1994.

6. *Arrangement of Verses (Padyaracanā)* of Lakṣmaṇabhaṭṭa Aṇkolakara: *Padyaracanā*. Edited by Jagannath Pathak. Allahabad: Ganganatha Jha Kendriya Sanskrit Vidyapitha, 1979.
7. *Ascent of King Kapphina (Kapphiṇābhyudaya)* of Śivasvāmin: *Śivasvāmin's Kapphiṇābhyudaya or Exaltation of King Kapphiṇa*. Edited by Gauri Shankar and Michael Hahn. New Delhi: Aditya Prakashan, 1989.
8. *Atharva Veda (Atharvaveda): Gli Inni dell'Atharvaveda (Saunaka)*. Edited by Chatia Orlandi. Vol. 28. Orientamenti Linguistici. Pisa: Giardini, 1991.
9. Balram Shukla is a professor of Sanskrit at the University of Delhi. Verses are unpublished.
10. *Bawd's Counsel (Kuṭṭanīmata)* of Damodaragupta: *Dāmodaraguptaviracitaṃ Kuṭṭanīmataṃ: The Bawd's Counsel*. Edited and translated by Dominic Goodall and Csaba Dezso. Vol. XXIII. Groningen Oriental Studies. Groningen: Egbert Forsten, 2012.
11. *Bhartrihari's Three Hundred (Śatakatraya)* of Bhartṛhari: *The Epigrams Attributed to Bhartṛhari*. Edited by D.D. Kosambi. Vol. 23. Singhi Jain Series. Bombay: Bharatiya Vidya Bhavan, 1948.
12. *Bhartrisarasvata's Anthology (Sūktāvali)* of Bhartṛsārasvata. Unpublished. Shree Raghunath Sanskrit Research Institute Library, Jammu. Ms 757. An unsatisfactory edition of the Śṛṅgāra section was published by Chr. Lindtner in 1993.
13. *Bihari's Seven Hundred (Satsai)* of Biharilal: *Poems from the Satsai.* Translated by Rupert Snell. Murty Classical Library of India. Harvard University Press, 2021.

14. *Birth of Kumara (Kumārasambhava)* of Kālidāsa: *Vallabhadeva's Kommentar (Śāradā-Version) Zum Kumārasambhava Des Kālidāsa*. Edited by M.S. Narayana Murti and Klaus L. Janert. Wiesbaden: Franz Steiner Verlag, 1980.
15. *Blazing Flames (Ujjvalajvālā)* of Śatāvadhāṇī R. Ganesh: Śatāvadhāṇiracanāsañcayanaṃ. Compiled and edited by Balram Shukla. New Delhi: Sahitya Akademi, 2019.
16. *Bundle on Love (Kāmasamūha)* of Anantakavi: *Kāma Samūha of Srī Anant Kavi: Text with English Translation, Critical Introduction, and Appendices*. Edited and translated by Amal Shib Pathak. Vol. 11. Mohandas Indological Series. New Delhi: Chaukhambha Publications, 2008.
17. *Cloud Messenger (Meghadūta)* of Kālidāsa: *The Meghadûta of Kâlidâsa: With the Commentary (Saṃjîvanî) of Mallinâtha*. Edited and translated into English by M.R. Kale. Bombay: Gopal Narayeṇ & Co., 1947.
18. *Collection of Gahas (Subhāsiagāhāsaṃgaha)*: 'Subhāsiagāhāsaṃgaho'. In *Jineśvarasūri's Gāhārayaṇakoso*, 52:67–75. L.D. Series. Ahmedabad: L.D. Institute of Indology, 1975.
19. *Collection of Prakrit Verse (Subhāsiapajjasaṃgaha)*: 'Subhāsiapajjasaṃgaho'. In *Jineśvarasūri's Gāhārayaṇakoso*, 52:76–82. L.D. Series. Ahmedabad: L.D. Institute of Indology, 1975.
20. *Commentary on Kavyalankara (Kāvyālaṅkāraṭippaṇī)* of Namisādhu: *Kāvyālaṇkāra (a Treatise on Rhetoric) of Rudraṭa with the Commentary of Namisādhu*. Edited by Pandit Durgāprasāda and Kāśīnātha Pāṇḍuranga Paraba. Vol. 2. Kāvyamālā. Bombay: Nirnaya Sagar, 1886.
21. *Deeds of the Nishadha King (Naiṣadhīyacarita)* of Śrīharṣa: *Naiṣadhamahākāvya Saṭīka: Cāṇḍū Paṇḍita Kṛta*

Naiṣadhadīpikā Tīkā Sahita. Edited by Jayadeva Jānī and Ānandakumāra. Vol. 188. Rājasthana Purātana Granthamālā. Jodhpur: Rajasthan Oriental Research Institute, 1997.
22. *Discourse on the Buddha's Passing (Mahāparinibbānasutta)*: *The Dīgha Nikāya*, Vol. II. Edited by T.W. Rhys Davids and J. Estlin Carpenter. London: Pali Text Society, 1947.
23. *Enlivener of Connoisseurs (Rasikajīvana)* of Gadādharabhaṭṭa: *Gadādharabhaṭṭasaṇkalito Rasikajivanam Ityākhyaḥ Saṃskṛtapadyasaṅgrahaḥ*. Edited by Trilokanātha Jhā. Darabhanga: Mithilā-Saṃskṛta-Sodha-Saṃsthānam, 2010.
24. *Guide to Letter Writing (Lekhapaddhati): Lekhapaddhati*. Edited by Chimanlal D. Dalal. Vol. XIX. Gaekwad Oriental Series. Baroda: Central Library, 1925.
25. *Handful of Thorns (Kaṇṭakāñjali)* of Krishna S. Arjunwadkar: *Kaṇṭakārjunaviracitaḥ Kaṇṭakāñjaliḥ (Navanītiśatakaṃ)*. Authored and translated by Kaṇṭakārjuna (Krishna S. Arjunwadkar). Pune: Suresh Phadnis, S.P. Prints Agency, 2008.
26. *Hanuman's Play (Hanumannāṭaka): Śrīmaddhanumatā Viracitaṃ Hanumannāṭakam*. Edited by Dāmodaramiśra and Śivarāma Śāstrī Keḷakara. Kalyāṇa-Muṃbaī [i.e. Bombay]: Lakṣmīveṅkaṭeśvara Mudraṇāgāra, 1900.
27. *Hara's Girdle (Haramekhalā)* of Māhuka: *The Haramekhala of Māhuka with Sanskrit Commentary (Part I)*. Edited by K. Sāmbaśiva Śāstrī. Vol. CXXIV. Trivandrum Sanskrit Series. Trivandrum: Government Press, 1937.
28. Heard through the oral tradition.
29. *Heart's Delight (Mānasollāsa)* of Someśvara: *Mānasollāsa of King Someśvara Vol. III*. Edited by G.K. Shrigondekar. Vol. 138. Gaekwad's Oriental Series. Baroda: Oriental Institute, 1961.
30. *Husband and Wife Talk (Patipatnīsallāpa)* of G.S. Srinivasa Murthy: 'Patipatnīsaṃlāpaḥ', 22 July 2016. https://groups.

google.com/g/bvparishat/c/NgWCNRK6YY8/m/VK_ywcp0BwAJ

31. *Jasmine Garland (Kundamālā)* of Dhīranāga: *Kundamālā Mahākaviśrīdiṅnāgaviracitā.* Edited by Jayacandraśāstrī. Lahore: Motilala Banārasīdāsa, 1929.
32. *Joy of the Serpents (Nāgānanda)* of Harṣavardhana: *The Nâgânanda of Srî Harsha Deva with the Commentary Nâgânandavimarsinî by Sivarâma.* Edited by T. Ganapati Sâstrî. Trivandrum: Superintendent, Government Press, 1917.
33. *Kamasutra (Kāmasūtra)* of Vātsyāyana Mallanāga: *Śrīvātsyāyanapraṇītaṃ Kāmasūtram.* Edited by Pandit Durgāprasāda. 2nd Edition. Bombay: Nirnaya Sagar, 1900.
34. *Kumarapala's Awakening (Kumārapālapratibodha)* of Somaprabhācārya: *Śrīsomaprabhācāryaviracitaḥ Kumārapālapratibodhaḥ.* Edited by Jinavijaya. Vol. XIV. Gaekwad's Oriental Series. Baroda: Central Library, 1920.
35. *Kusha and Kumudvati (Kuśakumudvatīyanāṭaka)* of Atirātrayajvan: *Contribution of Atirātrayajvan to Sanskrit Literature. Includes the Text of Kuśakumudvatīyanāṭaka and Tripuravijayacampū.* Edited by Jayasree, S. Doctor of Philosophy, University of Madras. https://shodhganga.inflibnet.ac.in/handle/10603/280431
36. *Light on Love (Śṛṅgāraprakāśa)* of Bhoja: *Śṛṅgāraprakāśa [Sāhityaprakāśa] by Bhojarāja.* Edited by Rewāprasāda Dwivedī and Sadāśivakumāra Dwivedī. 2 vols. New Delhi: Indira Gandhi National Centre for the Arts and Kālidāsasamsthāna, 2007.
37. *Light on Suggestion (Dhvanyāloka)* of Ānandavardhana: *Śrīmadānandavardhanācāryapraṇīto Dhvanyālokaḥ.* Edited by Pandit Durgāprasāda, Kāśīnātha Paṇḍuraṅga Paraba, and Vāsudeva Lakṣmaṇa Śastrī Paṇaśīkara. Reprint of 1935

Nirnaya Sagar edition. New Delhi: Mushiram Manoharlal Publishers, 1983.

38. *Light on Ten Kinds of Drama (Daśarūpakāloka)* of Dhanika: *Śrīdhanañjayaviracitaṃ Daśarūpakaṃ Dhanikakṛtayāvalokākhyayā Vyākhyayā Sametam.* Edited by Kāśīnātha Pāṇḍuraṅga Paraba. Bombay: Nirnaya Sagar, 1897.
39. *Line-up of Good Verse (Subhāṣitāvalī)* of Vallabhadeva: *Subhāṣitāvaliḥ Śrīmadvallabhadevasaṅgṛhītā.* Edited by Peter Peterson and Pandit Durgāprasāda. Bombay: Bhāṇḍārakaraprācyavidyāmandiramudraṇālaya, 1886.
40. *Little Clay Cart (Mṛcchakaṭika)* of Śūdraka: *The Little Clay Cart by Shúdraka.* Translated by Diwakar Acharya. Clay Sanskrit Library. New York: New York University Press: JJC Foundation, 2009.
41. *Madhavanala and Kamakandala (Mādhavānalākhyāna)* of Ānandadhara: 'Kavi Ānandadharaviracita Mādhavānalākhyānam'. In *Mādhavānala-Kāmakandalā Prabandha*, Vol. I, XCIII: 341–501. Gaekwad's Oriental Series. Baroda: Oriental Institute, 1942.
42. *Mahabharata (Mahābhārata)* of Vyāsa: Electronic text of the critical edition of the Mahabharata published by Bhandarkar Oriental Research Institute, Pune. Input by Muneo Tokunaga and revised by John Smith. https://bombay.indology.info/mahabharata/statement.html
43. *Malati and Madhava (Mālatīmādhava)* of Bhavabhūti: *Mālatīmādhava of Bhavabhūti with the Commentary Rasamañjarī of Pūrṇasarasvatī.* Edited by K.S. Mahādeva Śāstrī. Vol. 170. Trivandrum Sanskrit Series. Trivandrum: Government Central Press, 1953.
44. *Mallikamakaranda (Mallikāmakarandanāṭaka)* of Rāmacandrasūri: *Rāmacandra's Mallikāmakarandanāṭaka.*

Edited by Punyavijayaji. Vol. 91. L.D. Series. Ahmedabad: L.D. Institute of Indology, 1983.

45. *Mirror of Poetry (Kāvyādarśa)* of Daṇḍin: *Kavyalakṣaṇa of Daṇḍin (also Known as Kāvyādarśa) with Commentary Called Ratnaśrī of Ratnaśrījñāna*. Edited by Anantalal Thakur and Upendra Jha. Darbhanga: Mithila Institute of Post-Graduate Studies and Research in Sanskrit Learning, 1957.
46. *Munichandra's Gaha Treasury (Rasāulagāhākosa)* of Municandra: Unpublished. Bhandarkar Oriental Research Institute Ms. 791 in the Catalogue of 1899–1915. Extracts have been published. 'Gathakosa by Municandrasûri'. In *Reports on a Search for Sanskrit Manuscripts with an Index of Books*, 297–302. Bombay: Society's Library, 1887.
47. *Ornament to Love (Śṛṅgāratilaka)*: *Kalidasae Meghaduta et Çringaratilaka*. Edited by Johann Gildemeister. Bonn: H.B. Konig, 1841.
48. *Pearl Necklace of Verses (Sūktimuktāvalī)* of Jalhaṇa: *The Sūktimuktāvalī of Bhagadatta Jalhaṇa*. Edited by Embar Krishnamacharya. Vol. LXXXII. Gaekwad's Oriental Series. Baroda: Oriental Institute, 1938.
49. *Princess Kadambari (Kādambarī)* of Bāṇa: *Kādambarī of Bāṇabhaṭta and His Son (Bhusaṇabhaṭṭa) with the Commentaries of Bhānucandra and His Disciple Siddhacandra. Includes the commentary Caṣaka of Mathurānātha Śāstrī.* Edited by Kāśīnātha Pānḍurang Parab. Bombay: Satyabhāmābāī Pāṇḍurañg (for Nirnaya Sagar), 1948.
50. *Princess Karpuramanjari (Karpūramañjarī)* of Rājaśekhara: *Karpūramañjarī by Kavirāja Rājaśekhara*. Edited and translated by N.G. Suru. Bombay: N.G. Suru, Principal, Ruparel College, 1960.
51. *Princess Kuvalayamala (Kuvalayamālā)* of Uddyotanasūri: *Uddyotana-Sūri's Kuvalayamālā (a Unique Campu in*

Prakrit). Part I. Edited by A.N. Upadhye. Vol. 45. Singhi Jain Series. Bombay: Bharatiya Vidya Bhavan, 1959.

52. *Princess Lilavai (Līlāvaī)* of Koūhala: *Lilavai*. Edited and translated into English by Andrew Ollett. Murty Classical Library of India. Harvard University Press, 2021.
53. *Princess Vasavadatta (Vāsavadattā)* of Subandhu: *Vāsavadattā*. Edited by Śṛīkṛṣṇaṣūri (R.V. Krishnamachariar). Śrīraṅganagara: Śrīvāṇīvilāsa Mudrāyantrālaya, 1906.
54. *Ramayana (Rāmāyaṇa)* of Vālmīki: *The Yuddhakāṇḍa: The Sixth Book of the Vālmīki-Rāmāyaṇa*. Critically edited by P.L. Vaidya. Baroda: Oriental Institute, Baroda, 1971.
55. *Rig Veda (Ṛgveda)*: *Die Hymnen Des Ṛigveda Herausgegeben von Theodor Aufrecht: Zweiter Theil Maṇḍala VII-X*. Edited by Theodor Aufrecht. Bonn: Adolph Marcus, 1877.
56. *Rogue and Rake Confer (Dhūrtaviṭasaṃvāda)* of Īśvaradatta: 'Rogue and Pimp Confer'. In *The Quartet of Causeries by Syamilaka, Vararuchi, Sudraka and Isvaradatta*. Edited and translated into English by Csaba Deszo and Somadeva Vasudeva. Clay Sanskrit Library. New York: New York University Press, 2009.
57. *Secrets of Pleasure (Ratirahasya)* of Kokkoka: *Ratirahasya of Kokkok. Edited with Dīpikā Sanskrit commentary of Kāñcīnātha and a self-composed Hindi commentary Prakāśa by Ramananda Sharma*. Varanasi: Krishnadas Academy, 1994.
58. *Seven Hundred Aryas (Āryāsaptaśatī)* of Govardhana: *Seven Hundred Elegant Verses by Govardhana*. Translated by Friedhelm Hardy. Clay Sanskrit Library. New York: New York University Press, 2009.
59. *Seven Hundred Gahas (Gāhāsattasaī)* of Hāla: *Das Saptaçatakam Des Hâla*. Edited by Albrecht Weber. Leipzig: Brockhaus, 1881

60. *Sharngadhara's Anthology (Śārṅgadharapaddhati)* of Śārṅgadhara: *Śārṅgadhara Paddhati: Being an Anthology of Sanskrit Verses*. Reprint of Peter Peterson's 1888 Bombay Edition. Edited by Peter Peterson. Delhi: Chaukhamba Sanskrit Pratishthan, 1987.
61. *Slaying of Ravana (Rāvaṇavaho)* of Pravarasena: *Pravarasena's Rāvaṇavaha-Mahākāvyam with the Commentary of Setu-Tattva-Candrikā*. Edited by Radhagovinda Basak. Vol. VIII. Calcutta Sanskrit College Research Series. Calcutta: Sanskrit College, 1959.
62. *Slaying of the King of Gauda (Gauḍavaho)* of Vākpatirāja: *Gaüḍavaho by Vākpatirāja*. Edited and translated into English by N.G. Suru. Vol. 18. Prakrit Text Series. Ahmedabad: Prakrit Text Society, 1975.
63. *Sundari and Nanda (Saundarānanda)* of Aśvaghoṣa: *The Saundarananda of Aśvaghoṣa*. Critically edited by E.H. Johnston. London: Oxford University Press for the University of Panjab, Lahore, 1928.
64. *Tales of Bhoja (Bhojaprabandha)* of Ballālasena: *The Bhojaprabandha of Ballala*. Edited by Vāsudeva Śarma Paṇaśīkara. 10th Edition. Bombay: Nirnaya Sagar, 1932.
65. *Tales of Ten Young Men (Daśakumāracarita)* of Daṇḍin: *What Ten Young Men Did by Dandin*. Translated by Isabelle Onians. Clay Sanskrit Library. New York: New York University Press-JJC Foundation, 2005.
66. *The Kick (Pādatāḍitaka)* of Śyāmilaka: 'The Kick'. In *The Quartet of Causeries by Syamilaka, Vararuchi, Sudraka and Isvaradatta*. Edited and translated into English by Csaba Deszo and Somadeva Vasudeva. Clay Sanskrit Library. New York: New York University Press, 2009.
67. *The Lotus Gift (Padmaprābhṛtaka)* of Śūdraka: 'The Lotus Gift'. In *The Quartet of Causeries by Syamilaka, Vararuchi,*

Sudraka and Isvaradatta. Edited and translated into English by Csaba Deszo and Somadeva Vasudeva. Clay Sanskrit Library. New York: New York University Press, 2009.

68. *Thief's Fifty Verses (Caurapañcāśikā)* of Bilhaṇa: *Phantasies of a Love Thief: The Caurapañcāśikā Attributed to Bilhaṇa*. Critically edited and translated into English by Barbara Stoler Miller. Vol. 6. Studies in Oriental Culture. New York and London: Columbia University Press, 1971.
69. *Treasury of Gahas (Gāhārayaṇakoso)* of Jineśvarasūri: *Jineśvarasūri's Gāhārayaṇakoso*. Edited by Amritlal M. Bhojak and Nagin J. Shah. Vol. 52. L.D. Series. Ahmedabad: L.D. Institute of Indology, 1975.
70. *Treasury of Verse-Jewels (Subhāṣitaratnakośa)* of Vidyākara: *The Subhāṣitaratnakoṣa*. Edited by D.D. Kosambi and V.V. Gokhale. Vol. 42. Harvard Oriental Series. Cambridge, Massachusetts: Harvard University Press, 1957.
71. *Urvashi Won by Valour (Vikramorvaśīya)* of Kālidāsa: *The Vikramorvaśīya of Kālidāsa*. Critically edited by H.D. Velankar. New Delhi: Sahitya Akademi, 1961.
72. *Vajjalagga (Vajjālagga)* of Jayavallaha: *Jayavallabha's Vajjālaggam with the Sanskrit Commentary of Ratnadeva*. Edited and translated into English by M.V. Patwardhan. Vol. 14. Prakrit Text Society Series. Ahmedabad: Prakrit Text Society, 1969.
73. *Vidyakara Mishra's Thousand (Vidyākarasahasraka)* of Vidyākaramiśra: *Vidyakara-Sahasrakam: Anthology of Sanskrit Verses*. Edited by Umesha Mishra. Vol. II. Sanskrit Series. Allahabad: Allahabad University Publications, 1942.
74. *Warehouse of Verses (Subhāṣitaratnabhāṇḍāgāra)* of N.R. Acharya: *Subhāṣita-Ratna-Bhāṇḍāgāra or Gems of Sanskrit Poetry Being a Collection of Witty, Epigrammatic, Instructive and Descriptive Verses with Their Sources*. 8th Edition. Edited by Nārāyaṇ Rām Āchārya. Bombay: Nirnaya Sagar, 1952.

75. *Ways of the Madam (Samayamātṛkā)* of Kṣemendra: *Samayamātrikā of Kshemendra*. Edited by Pandit Durgāprasād and Kāśīnātha Pāndurang Parab. Vol. 10. Kāvyamālā. Bombay: Nirnaya Sagar, 1925.
76. *Wedding of Kadambari (Kādambarīkalyāṇanāṭaka)* of Narasiṃha: *Narasiṃhakaviviracitaṃ Kādambarīkalyāṇaṃ Nāṭakam*. Edited by Ve Kṛṣṇamācārya. Madras: Madrapurī eḍukeṣanal pabliṣiṅ samiti, 1936.
77. *Wedding of Subhadra (Subhadrāpariṇaya)* of Sudhīndratīrtha: *Śrīmatsudhīndratīrthaśrīpādaiḥ viracitaṃ Subhadrāpariṇayaṃ nāma Nāṭakam*. Edited by Gururājācārya and Sāṇūru Bhīmabhaṭṭa. Includes a Sanskrit commentary, 'Laghuvivaraṇa', by Sumatīndratīrtha. Beṅgalūru: Śrīparimalasaṃśodhanaprakāśanamandiraṃ, 1993.
78. *What Navasahasanka Did (Navasāhasāṅkacarita)* of Padmagupta: *Navasâhasâṇka Charita of Padmagupta Alias Parimala*. Part I: Containing the Preface, the Text with Various Readings and an Index to the ślokas. Edited by Vâmana Shastri Islâmpurkar. Bombay: Government Central Book Depot, 1895.
79. *What Rama Did Next (Uttararāmacarita)* of Bhavabhūti: *Rama's Last Act by Bhavabhuti*. Edited and translated into English by Sheldon Pollock. Clay Sanskrit Library. New York: New York University Press-JJC Foundation, 2007.
80. *Wishing Stone of Stories (Prabandhacintāmaṇi)* of Merutuṅga: *Prabandha Cintāmaṇi of Merutuṅgācārya*. Edited by Jinavijaya Muni. Vol. 1. Singhi Jain Series. Bombay: Bharatiya Vidya Bhavan, 1933.
81. *Wishing Tree of Rasa (Rasakalpadruma)* of Caturbhujamiśra: *Ācāryaśrīcaturbhujamiśraviracitasya Rasakalpadrumasya Samīkṣātmakaṃ Sampādanam*. Edited and translated into Hindi by Bhāskaramiśra. Delhi: Eastern Book Linkers, 1991.

List of All Examined Sources

Anthologies: Sabhyālaṇkaraṇa, Sūktisuṅdara, Rasikajīvana, Subhāṣitaratnakośa, Kāvyasaṅgraha (John Haberlin), Saduktikarṇāmṛta, Subhāṣitāvalī, Subhāṣitaratnabhāṇḍāgāra, Padyaveṇī, Sūktimuktāvalī, Śārṅgadharapaddhati, Kāmasamūha, Hariharasubhāṣita, Sūktimuktāvalī of Lakṣmaṇa, Vidyākarasahasraka, Padyāmṛtataraṅgiṇī, Padyāvalī, Sūktigaṅgādhara, Mahābhāratavacanāmṛta (Charudeva Shastri), Sūktiratnahāra, Śubhāṣitamuktāvalī (Ed. R.N. Dandekar), Padyaracanā, Subhāṣitasudhānidhi, Rasakalpadruma, Sūktiratnakoṣa of Lakṣmaṇa, Sūktimañjari (Baladeva Upadhyaya), Kālidāsa Apocrypha, Bhartṛhari's triśatī (D.D. Kosambi's critical edition), Śṛṅgāratilaka

Prakrit: Haramekhalā, Prākṛtasarvasva, Svayambhūchandas, Candralekhā of Rudradāsa, Chappaṇṇayagāhākosa, Gāhārayaṇakoso, Gāhāsattasaī (Albrecht Weber), Rambhāmañjarī, Vajjālagga, Rasāulagāhākoso of Municandra (unpublished), Alaṃkāradappaṇa, Suhāsiapajjasaṃgaho, Suhāsiagāhāsaṃgaho,

Kuvalayamālā, Karpūramañjarī, Prakrit Verses in Alankara Works (V.M. Kulkarni), Līlāvai, Kumārapālapratibodha.

Mahākavya: Madhurāvijaya, Kapphiṇābhyudaya, Navasāhasāṇkacarita, Rāmacarita, Setubandha, Rāvanavaho, Buddhacarita, Rāmāyaṇa, Saundarānanda, Jānakīharaṇa, Raghuvamśa, Naiṣadhīya, Kirātārjuniya, Śiśupālavadha, Kumārasambhava.

Nāṭaka: Udāttarāghava, Subhadrāpariṇaya of Sudīndratīrtha, Kaumudīmitrānanda, Nalavilāsa, Veṇīsaṃhāra, Pradyumnābhyudaya, Kādambarīnāṭaka, Mallikāmāruta of Uddaṇda, Hanumannāṭaka, Prabodhacandrodaya, Āgamaḍambara, Mudrārākṣasa, Mṛcchakaṭika, Anargharāghava, Nāgānanda, Ratnāvalī, Mallikāmarandanāṭaka, Caturbhāṇi, Kuśakumudvatīyanāṭaka, Abhijñānaśākuntala, Uttararāmacarita, Mālatīmādhava, Vikramorvaśīya, Mālavikāgnimitra, Kundamālā

Gadya: Kādambarī, Vāsavadattā, Daśakumāracarita, Śṛṅgāramañjarī of Bhoja.

Kāmaśāstra: Ratiratnapradīpikā, Kāmasūtra, Ratiramaṇa, Ratiśāstra, Ratirahasya, Kāmasūtra.

Apabhraṃśa: Hemaśabdānuśāsana, Sandeśarāsaka.

Campū: Varadāmbikāpariṇaya, Viśvaguṇādarśa, Jātakamālā of Haribhaṭṭa, Nalacampū, Udayasundarīkathā, Tilakamañjarī, Yaśastilaka.

Other Kāvya: Haṃsadūta of Vāmanabhaṭṭabāṇa, Rāmakarṇarasāyanaṃ of Rāmabhadra Dīkṣita, Kuṭṭanīmata,

Samayamātṛkā, Śṛṅgāravilāsa of Paṇḍitarāja Jagannatha, Āryāsaptaśatī, Śṛṅgārahārāvalī of Śrīharṣa, Contribution of Women to Sanskrit literature (Chaudhuri), Narmamālā, Āryāsaptaśatī of Viśveśvara, Sūktāvalī of Bhartṛsārasvata, Kokilasandeśa, Meghadūta, Dhoyi's Pavanadūta, Vedantadeśika's Hamsasandeśa, Mādhavānala-kāmakandala, Kaliviḍambana, Deśopadeśa, Darpadalana, Amaruśataka (Nirnaya Sagar edition), Kṛṣṇakarṇāmṛta, Kokilasandeśa of Uddaṇḍa, Bhojaprabandha, Caurapañcāśikā, Prabandhacintāmaṇi.

Alaṇkāra/Nāṭya: Kāvyādarśa, Dhvanyāloka, Śṛṅgārasaraṇi, Bhāvaprakāśana of Śāradātanaya, Rasaratnapradīpa, Śṛṅgāraprakāśa, Śṛṇgāramañjarī, Vakroktijīvita, Kāvyaprakāśa, Daśarūpaka, Rasamañjarī, Rasataraṅginī, Kuvalayānanda, Alaṇkārasarvasva, Rasārṇavasudhākara, Rasakalikā, Rasadīrghikā, Kāvyānuśāsana of Hemacandra.

Modern Sanskrit: Anārkali (V. Raghavan), Kaṇṭakāñjali (K.S. Arjunwadkar), Patipatnīsallāpa (G.S.S. Murty), Śatāvadhāniracanāsañcayanam (Shatavadhani R. Ganesh).

Others: Therīgāthā, Varāṅgacarita, Mānasollāsa, Rig Veda, Atharva Veda, Major Upanishads, Tipiṭaka, Lekhapaddhati.

Anusha Rao is a scholar of Sanskrit and Indian religion who likes writing new things about very old things. She is currently pursuing a PhD at the University of Toronto, and writes a column in the *Deccan Herald* presenting witty Sanskrit-flavoured takes on contemporary issues.

Suhas Mahesh is a scholar of Sanskrit and Prakrit with a terrible weakness for good verse, rare manuscripts and arcane grammar. By day, Suhas is a materials physicist with a PhD from the University of Oxford where he was a Rhodes Scholar.

Anusha and Suhas live in Toronto and would be happy to hear from readers at anushasrao310@gmail.com and suhas.msh@gmail.com. You can also leave a message at loveinsanskrit.com

HarperCollins *Publishers* India

At HarperCollins India, we believe in telling the best stories and finding the widest readership for our books in every format possible. We started publishing in 1992; a great deal has changed since then, but what has remained constant is the passion with which our authors write their books, the love with which readers receive them, and the sheer joy and excitement that we as publishers feel in being a part of the publishing process.

Over the years, we've had the pleasure of publishing some of the finest writing from the subcontinent and around the world, including several award-winning titles and some of the biggest bestsellers in India's publishing history. But nothing has meant more to us than the fact that millions of people have read the books we published, and that somewhere, a book of ours might have made a difference.

As we look to the future, we go back to that one word—a word which has been a driving force for us all these years.

Read.